# UNDERSTANDING
# THE CHRISTIAN FAITH

# UNDERSTANDING
## the
# CHRISTIAN FAITH

## Georgia Harkness

ABINGDON
*Nashville*

MANUFACTURED BY THE PARTHENON PRESS AT
NASHVILLE, TENNESSEE, UNITED STATES OF AMERICA

# ACKNOWLEDGMENTS

I AM INDEBTED to the editors of *The Christian Century*, *The Christian Advocate*, *Child Guidance in Christian Living*, and *The Link* for permission to reprint some portions of articles which have appeared in these periodicals. Two of my classes in "The Theology of the Lay Mind" at Garrett Biblical Institute have given me pointers in the direction of greater simplicity and clearness. My friends Dr. Ernest Fremont Tittle and Rev. Emmett W. Gould have read the manuscript and made useful suggestions. I am grateful to my friend Miss Verna Miller for very helpful co-operation in preparing this book for publication and giving me constant encouragement in the project. Beyond these whose assistance is direct and tangible, I am indebted to all the teachers of religion I ever had, all the students I ever taught, and to some—not all—of the books I have read.

# CONTENTS

# CONTENTS

# INTRODUCTION

*I*N BUSINESS IT is the consumer for whom goods are produced, and his acceptance or rejection determines—if not the quality of the goods—at least their ability to satisfy his wants. Accordingly, large amounts not only of money but of intelligence and artistic talent are thought well expended if through billboard, radio, or press the potential purchaser can be shown what the product is and does. In reference to what one shall eat, or drink, or put on, there is constant and varied education of the public.

In the churches it is the layman, not the theologian in the seminary or even the minister, who is the ultimate consumer for whom churches exist. What goes out from the pulpit or press must somehow get to the layman if the common people, who heard Jesus gladly, are to hear his message in our time. Since religion deals with something far more vital to man's welfare and happiness than the latest processed foods or styles in clothing, at least as much care ought to be taken to educate the public as to its stock in trade. But do we find it so? The rarity of any clear understanding of what the Christian faith is or what it means gives answer.

To shift the analogy from commerce to culture, the libraries and the newsstands are full of popular expositions of science. The "story" of philosophy and the "outlines" of history, literature, music, and art are available in most small-town libraries. Profound political issues are treated simply, not always polemically, in many books and magazines. There is no corresponding presentation of theology.

Is this because laymen are not interested in theology? There are doubtless many who think they are not. But if one listens carefully to any informal discussion of life and its problems—whether in church, club, dormitory, barracks, or living room—one is certain to hear theological issues raised before the discussion gets very far. Why is there all this misery in the world? Why do good people have to suffer when they don't deserve it? Does it do any good to pray? If there is a God, why didn't he prevent the war? Was it right to use the atomic bomb to stop it? What are we coming to? Is the end of the world coming soon? Do you expect to go to heaven when you die? Anyway, what is heaven? Where is it, if it isn't up in the sky? Will sinners burn in hell? With all this hell on earth, isn't Christianity a beautiful but impractical ideal? What is the difference between a Christian and any other decent person? What does it mean to be saved by Christ? Was Jesus divine in any way that we are not? Can you believe everything in the Bible? What are you going to do when religion and science conflict? Does the Church have any real message? Start in almost any way, and the conversation comes around to these and other theological questions.

"Theology" means "the study of God." It is a systematic attempt to understand what God is and does, how he is related to the world and to ourselves. It views life from the standpoint of Christian faith and attempts to say what a Christian may believe about such questions as those raised in the last paragraph. There is, of course, no answer that is acceptable at every point to all Christians. God has not run his truth, or our minds, into a single mold. Yet there is a great body of common Christian convictions, and it is with these that we shall be mainly concerned in this book.

Theology is basic to religion, for while it is not the whole of religion, an emotional experience has no firm rootage without it. There can be no Christian faith without belief in something. If one believes the wrong things, his entire life can be distorted, for the world is so made that a firm structure of personal living can rest only on true foundations. And if one does not know what to believe among many conflicting possibilities, one may be left permanently unsettled and unnourished —like Buridan's ass that starved to death between two equally attractive bales of hay.

Serious consequences have arisen from failure to help the layman understand his faith. In the first place, grave personal problems have been created, or have found no solution when life presented them. To illustrate, many people can no longer pray because to them a personal God means an old man with a beard (visually conceived as a mixture of Moses, Santa Claus, and Father Time), and this God of their childhood has evaporated with nothing in its place but an impersonal principle. By others prayer has been abandoned because a too-literal faith that "with God all things are possible" has ended in frustration and bitterness. The ever-present problem of suffering, even if unsolved, could be more wisely as well as more bravely met if there were not so large a blank after the questions that accompany it. Bereaved persons, wistfully eager to believe in immortality, have a right to know on what foundations the Christian hope rests. Far more widely than it is comfortable to think, sincere Christians have had the spiritual life undercut by wrong answers, or no answer, to the basic questions of human existence.

Lack of clear understanding of the Christian faith stands in the way of an effective attack on the evils of our society. Laymen make the greater part of the political, economic, and social decisions on which human destinies depend. There are enough Christian laymen in the world to establish "peace on earth, good will among men" if laymen understood the Christian gospel and acted upon it. Knowledge alone will not guarantee right action, but lack of understanding can scatter and weaken Christian action until it fails to be very different from that of the secular world. This is illustrated by the lack of any clear principle on which lay opinions are held regarding such vital matters as the control of atomic energy, treatment of vanquished enemies, peacetime conscription, the settlement of labor disputes, the right of the Negro to fair conditions of employment. The more fully one understands the Christian gospel, the less his mind is prey to the newspaper, the radio, and the conversation he hears around him.

Everywhere are persons—some who are Christians, others interested inquirers—who would seriously like to know what a Christian may believe about God, and Christ, and prayer, and sin, and suffering, and salvation, and death, and destiny. It is for these that this book is written. Let no one suppose that it will give all the answers, or do one's thinking for him! Its purpose is to set forth the basic Christian convictions for the *lay*, not for the *lame*, mind.

An attempt will be made throughout to use simple and nontechnical language. I hope it is not presumptuous to expect that anyone who can read the *Saturday Evening Post* or the *Reader's Digest* can read and understand this book if he wants to! However, I do not feel called upon to fight shy of theological terms, as if they were something too old-fashioned to be mentioned in an enlightened scientific age. Most of them, such as judgment, redemption, incarnation, atonement, forgiveness, and grace, carried for our forefathers, along with some error, a vital truth which needs to be recovered and reinterpreted for our time. They belong in the great tradition of Christian theology, and instead of avoiding them through fear of misunderstanding, it has seemed better to try to say what they mean.

In order to make the book as brief as possible, it has been necessary in every chapter to pass rapidly over great issues. It has seemed more useful to say something about nearly all of the great Christian doctrines, and thus to enable the reader to see them together, than to linger at length over any. For the reader who wants a more extended study—and it is hoped that many will—other works are available.[1]

A further word is in order before the reader starts his quest. As to *know* a person is something richer and more full of meaning than to *know about him,* so in theology it is only as one seeks consciously to relate his life to God and obey his moral demands that one is able to grasp sympathetically the truth about him. This book is not for the curiously critical. It is for the open-minded seeker who, not expecting all mysteries to be revealed, is willing to live by the light he has while he seeks for more. The Christian faith is both a way of belief and a way of life. He who does not seek to know God for himself will not find him in the pages of this book—or any other.

[1] Attention is called to the Selected Bibliography at the end of the book, where both simple and more advanced treatments of theology are listed.

## Chapter I

## THE MEANING OF FAITH

*F*AITH IS BASIC to Christianity. The word appears so often in the New Testament that the allusions come crowding close upon one another:

Now faith is assurance of things hoped for, a conviction of things not seen.

... who through faith subdued kingdoms, wrought righteousness, obtained promises, stopped the mouths of lions, quenched the power of fire, escaped the edge of the sword, from weakness were made strong, waxed mighty in war, turned to flight armies of aliens.

Being therefore justified by faith, we have peace with God through our Lord Jesus Christ.

Thy faith hath made thee whole.

According to your faith be it done unto you.

This is the victory that overcometh the world, even our faith.

In all these passages there is the note of assurance, active commitment, resolute conquest. With millions of people inwardly shaken and afraid, faith is one of the major requirements for social stability in our time. But in every time, however outwardly peaceful and serene the situation, man must have faith in order to live with inner poise and adequacy. What, then, *is* faith?

## I. *What faith is not*

It often happens that wrong ideas as to what faith involves create confusion and lead to false expectations. In order to go forward without obstruction, let us clear away the underbrush by asking first what faith is not.

To have faith does not mean to be gullible. Faith is not believing on inadequate evidence or with the evidence pointing in the opposite direction. In religion, as in other things, if one tries to believe something "by main strength and awkwardness," the believer's position is awkward but not strong. No intelligent person would believe everything he reads in the newspapers, including the claims of the patent medicine advertisements to cure all ailments! So in religion one must use discretion, not supposing that the demands of faith require him to believe everything that may be set forth in pious words.

The assumption that what we take on faith we take with closed minds, as if we had blinders on to shut out whatever light might creep in from other sources, lies at the root of the quarrel between religion and science. This is also the main source of the personal inner turmoil that sometimes results from shifting the base of one's religious thinking to new foundations. Much trouble would be saved by getting it clearly in mind at the outset that religious ideas, like any other ideas, can be true only when they are tied to reality and tested by the whole of life.

In the second place, though faith is related to belief, faith is never wholly a matter of intellectual assent to the truth of a statement. One can believe in God with a very complete set of arguments, yet not have any faith that makes a difference in living. On the other hand, with a minimum of intellectual foundations—though always with *some*—one may have a powerful faith. One's belief ought to be as near right as hard thinking and inquiry will make it, for otherwise faith though strong is apt to be inflexible and misdirected. But it is a mistake to suppose that when we discover we must alter some belief, our faith will collapse. To illustrate, one's faith in God need not vanish when he outgrows the idea that God is a kind-faced elderly gentleman in the sky. Faith in God the Creator does not stand or fall with a particular belief about the processes of creation, as many can testify who without loss of faith have exchanged belief in a six-day creation for the larger vision of a God who through many millions of years has been fashioning his universe.

And in the third place, faith is not identical with mystery—a deep, dark reservoir into which to dump anything that seems unexplainable. The danger of this view lies in the fact that on this basis the more knowledge we get, the more our faith recedes. There is, and probably always will be, some mystery about the things of faith. We "see through a glass darkly," as Paul put it, regarding many things. Yet it is not the darkness or the light that determines the presence of faith; it is what we do with either one when we find ourselves in the midst of it.

## 2. *What faith is*

Faith, then, does not mean belief without any basis, or intellectual assent to certain ideas, or a leap from solid footing into a chasm of mystery. But what does it mean?

It means, first, *positive trust* in somebody or something, the willingness to commend one's life to another's keeping or to act on some conviction believed to be true. The familiar definition, "Faith is *assurance* of things hoped for, a *conviction* of things not seen," [1] brings out this meaning. Go through all the biblical statements quoted above, and there is not one of them that does not emphasize this active, positive aspect, both in the exercise of faith and in its fruits.

Some analogies on the human level will make clearer what religious faith entails. One does not eat his dinner or lie down on his bed at night without faith that the food will nourish and not poison him, that the bed will support and not suffocate him. One does not usually go to a doctor unless he has faith that the doctor will help him get well. One does not—or ought not—to marry

[1] Hebrews 11:1.

18

without faith that the other person will co-operate to form a home. In all these instances suspicion can undermine faith, and it ought to undermine it if there are valid grounds for mistrust. Otherwise one is credulous rather than trusting. But if we distrust where we ought to have faith, we not only make ourselves and others unhappy but we cut ourselves off from bodily health and enrichment of spirit. Life could not go on fruitfully without a large-scale exercise of faith in our everyday social relations.

Transfer this principle to our relation to God, and what do we find? The basic atheism is not intellectual rejection of belief in God's existence. If one cares enough to question about God, there is far more hope for him than if he is indifferent. As Tennyson put it:

> There lives more faith in honest doubt,
> Believe me, than in half the creeds.

The basic atheism is unwillingness to commit our lives to God's keeping, callousness to God's demands, the ordering of life as if God did not exist. This is the "sin of unbelief," a lack of faith so widespread in our time that society has been honeycombed by it and engulfed in world-wide destruction. To have faith in God is not merely to assert that God exists (which few people dispute) but to do the much harder thing of putting our trust in God and his way as the basis for individual and social living.

19

This suggests a second meaning, that of *courageous adventure*. Indeed courage is presupposed in faith as trust and commitment, for while there are some things to which to commit ourselves without incurring risk, this is not true of many things of importance. To get married, or choose a vocation, or give oneself to a cause is to act on faith—not blindly, but with full awareness that difficulties as well as delights are in store. We must count the cost and be willing to pay it before we can go ahead. To "walk by faith and not by sight" does not mean to stumble around in the dark, but with many of the details hidden to go forward boldly by the light we have.

Though faith of this kind is required in the whole of life, it is particularly true in religion that we must resolve courageously to act if faith is to deliver us from lethargy and despair. To be a Christian is to seek to do the will of God at all costs. Yet it often happens that the harder we try, the more we feel cramped by failure. We must have help, or give up in defeat. In short, we must be "saved by faith" if we are to act in faith.

But what does it mean to be "saved by faith"? Part of it is man's trusting and obedient response to God, of which we have been speaking. But before we can respond, God must have acted. So a third meaning of faith appears.

Saving faith means *saving help*—an experience in which one feels that light and strength and the joy of victory over temptation flow into his life from God.

Submitting one's life in confident assurance to God, obedient as far as one is able but still unable to master himself, one feels lifted by a power not his own. A sensitive Christian never ceases to wonder at the mystery and marvel of inflowing power that comes, all undeserved, from God's gracious love. It was this new life coming from God to man in spite of his sin and unworthiness that led Luther and Calvin, and has led their modern followers, to speak of faith not as a human achievement but as God's gift. When one testifies to being saved by faith, or says that he has peace in his spirit because he is "justified by faith," what is meant is a life-giving power, channeled from God to man and not merely brought about by our human effort. To join the church "on confession of faith" ought to signify such an experience of newness of life imparted by God to a receptive soul.

Faith then means confident trust, courageous adventure, and an inflowing of God-given power. But has it nothing to do with truth? It has a great deal. This leads us to a fourth meaning, which we might call *illumined belief.*

It is faith that enables us to have eyes to see and ears to hear. It is faith as "insight" that quickens the mind to truer "sight." As one learns the truth about science only when his eyes are opened by an eagerness that drives him to learn, as one really sees great art or listens to great music only when his soul is sensitive to it, as one finds depths of richness in a friend only through

21

an outgoingness of spirit that opens new channels, so one learns the truth about God only when he "stands in faith." One may get a detached sort of knowledge, which is true enough as far as it goes, by a weighing of arguments and canvassing of evidence as to the existence and nature of God. One does not really get to Christian faith until he lets God capture his spirit. Then, with no setting aside of the mind and its faculties but with a wiser use of them, we can move upward toward truth, outward toward victory over the world, inward toward the faith that makes us whole.

This gives a clue to the relations of faith to reason, which are not so contradictory as they are sometimes assumed to be. Faith does not mean something that must overrule reason; nor does it mean something that must give way before reason. Faith and reason ought not to be kept in watertight compartments, as if one might overflow and put out the other's fire. Rather, they are to be regarded as two necessary and closely related approaches to life. The intellectual processes give us much valuable knowledge for which no amount of faith is a substitute; yet as vision and active commitment, faith is essential to all of life including the search for truth.

Our problem is not, "Shall we walk by faith?" Every man, whether he wants to or not, exercises faith in something every day that he lives. The real problems are: "What shall we have faith in?" and "How shall we have it?" Christian faith exists because Christianity has a conviction about God that gives, beyond everything else, assurance and power for living.

During England's darkest days in 1940, King George VI in his Christmas broadcast brought to the attention of the world some lines which express movingly the meaning of faith:

I said to a man who stood at the gate of the year, "Give me a light that I may tread safely into the unknown," and he replied, "Go out into the darkness and put your hand into the hand of God. That shall be to you better than a light and safer than a known way!"[3]

Faith is the union of trusting confidence and courageous action with response to God's leading, and of all these with the insight that lights the way toward truth. It is this combination that makes Christian faith such a powerful force. Our world, far from having outgrown it, desperately needs more. Faith is not all there is of religion, but without it we shall have neither saving hope nor conquering love.

[3] By M. Louise Haskins.

## Chapter II

# UNDERSTANDING THE BIBLE

*I*F ONE IS TO understand what is true about the Christian religion, he must read and understand the Bible. This is not to say there is no truth to be found elsewhere. God speaks through the marvelous orderliness and beauty of nature, and he speaks through great souls and the highest thoughts of men wherever they are found. Nevertheless, there is no substitute for this central source of our knowledge of God. This makes it imperative that we not only read the Bible, but read it with understanding.

It is one of the major defects of our culture that in the name of religious freedom the Bible has been kept out of the public schools. Children who ought to be as free to study it as to study Shakespeare have been deprived of getting any knowledge of it in school. An appalling biblical illiteracy has been creeping up on us for two generations, with the result that there is not now much biblical knowledge in the homes to impart to the children. Instruction in the Sunday schools is greatly limited in time and often in leadership, and week-day religious instruction on time released to the churches by the public schools has not yet become general. Though a passage of scripture is read in most Sunday morning services, biblical preaching is not much in vogue and the historical setting is seldom explained. The natural consequence of all this is that such meager biblical knowledge as most people have is tinctured with misinformation and often tied up with interpretations that go contrary, not only to scientific fact, but to the demands of Christian faith.

Ignorance tends to beget hostility or indifference. With either comes a loss of the positive direction for living which the Bible could impart. Though many things have converged to cause the loss of moral fiber which has led to our present social chaos, not the least is a general failure to grasp God's timeless message that is written in the Bible.

## 1. *Its devotional use*

It is necessary to distinguish at the outset between two related and equally necessary, but not identical, uses of the Bible. One should read it for devotional purposes—to find in it comfort and challenge, to be strengthened by it for a better meeting of life's daily demands. But one should read it also as one would study any other great book—for an understanding of its total structure, message, and contribution to truth. It is with the second of these uses that we are mainly concerned in this chapter.

Some suggestions are in order, however, as to the devotional use of the Bible, for the person who does not let his life be quickened by it is not apt to have the right perspective for understanding its ideas. For the most fruitful use in personal devotions one does not usually try to read a chapter a day regardless of what is in it, for not all parts of the Bible are on the same level of power. It is better to read it thoughtfully a few verses at a time and with a quiet receptive spirit let God speak to us through the meaning the words convey.

The choice of the passage to be read should follow some system to avoid the aimlessness of a random coursing around. But many systems are possible—the topical arrangement that goes with a devotional aid like *The Upper Room,* a cycle of readings on a single theme, an unhurried study of some book that is full of power. Among the latter the Gospels, Paul's letters, the psalms, and the writings of the great prophets are more likely to yield fruit than the endless genealogies of the book of Numbers, the minute legal prescriptions of Leviticus, or the cryptic symbolism of much of Revelation.

It is surprising how much new truth can leap out from even the most familiar passage. As one reads one should think about the meaning, raising questions if they come naturally but never allowing a snag to deflect attention from whatever positive message the words contain. One should read as one would a letter from a friend, with alertness but with sympathetic attention to the main thing the friend is saying rather than fussiness over just how it is said. Above all, one should read prayerfully and with the willingness to apply to one's own life whatever of comfort or of demand from God the words suggest.

Read in this spirit, the Bible even with all puzzles becomes what the Church at its best has always considered it—God's Word to men. It is a way in which God speaks to us to give assurance, power, and direction for living. Such personal acquaintance is essential to the Christian. But this is not all that is needed. To understand more fully what the Bible says, one must give to it the same patient, thorough, open-minded study that any other great piece of literature requires.

## 2. *Principles of interpretation*

If the truth in the Bible is to be arrived at, several principles must be observed as one reads and studies it.

First, one must remember that there is in it "heavenly treasure in earthen vessels." It is the record of God's dealings with men written over a span of at least a thousand years. It shows in many ways how God, who is "the high and holy One of Israel," dwells also in the hearts of the humble and contrite to condemn, direct, strengthen, and save his people. If inspiration is "inbreathing," as its basic meaning suggests,[1] the Bible is an inspired collection of literature, for it shows throughout the inbreathing of the divine spirit. Again, if anything is inspired which inspires in us great thoughts and noble feelings, as one is apt to say of an "inspired" work of art or music, the Bible is inspired beyond all other books because it has done most through the centuries to lift people to their best.

[1] From the Latin *inspiro*, "breath into."

But this is not to say that every word or passage in the Bible comes directly from God and is therefore not to be questioned. God did not dictate the Bible to the persons who wrote it, as one might give something to a stenographer! The authors who wrote the Bible—and many persons had a hand in writing parts of it—were human beings like ourselves and as prone to make mistakes. They were people who had experienced God in their own lives and who saw him working in the history of their people, and without ever expecting it to become holy scripture they wrote what they believed and felt. Many of their own erroneous ideas naturally got mixed in with the truth that came to them from God. In a day before any science was heard of, it was inevitable that unscientific ideas should appear in the writings. We cannot expect to find in the Old Testament all the high ethical insights of Jesus. Where there are several accounts of the same happening, the details differ. When descriptions of events were written down long after the events occurred, inaccuracies crept in. Yet the wonder is that in spite of these circumstances so much of sublime, God-given truth stands out from the pages of the Bible. It is the discovery of this truth in its setting of human weakness and error that makes the study of the Bible so rewarding and fascinating.

Second, we must read the Bible in its historical setting; that is, we must consider, regarding any book or passage, what the circumstances were which caused it to be written. This is the only way to get a true estimate of the author's meaning. Though it is impossible to give an exact date for most of the books, it is possible to know approximately when each was written, in what sequence they came, what the situation was in the life of the individual writer or his people that called it forth. A great deal of study has been done in the past hundred years to establish these facts and there is large agreement among scholars, though there are still problems enough so that the work is not finished. It is now certain that the books as they stand in the Bible do not represent their real order of writing and that the traditional authorship must in some cases be questioned. Since this is a highly technical study, most of us must take the results of such investigations secondhand. Yet as we learn even in an elementary way the historical background of each book, a flood of light is thrown on its message.[2]

Third, we must consider what kind of literature we have in each book. The Bible is not one book, but a library of sixty-six books. It contains almost every kind of literature there is—not history and moral precepts only, but poetry, drama, folklore, allegory, legal codes, genealogies, vital statistics, short stories, essays, sermons,

[2] Among the best popular guides for such understanding are H. E. Fosdick's *A Guide to the Understanding of the Bible*, E. J. Goodspeed's *The Story of the Bible*, W. R. Bowie's *The Story of the Bible*, and J. P. Love's *How to Read the Bible*. To these may be added, for the Old Testament, Julius Bewer's *The Literature of the Old Testament* and Fleming James' *Personalities of the Old Testament;* for the New Testament, Mary Ely Lyman's *The Christian Epic* and Albert Barnett's *The New Testament: Its Making and Meaning.*

letters, philosophy, prophecy, descriptive narration. It contains great passages about nature but no science, for the people who wrote it were not scientifically minded. It contains in some books much symbolism, though this does not justify us in trying to find hidden symbolic meanings throughout. By this "allegorical" method of interpretation much harm has been done, for people have read into the Bible their own ideas instead of finding what is there.

The way to get at the truth is to read each book or passage in the light of its purpose and literary style as well as in its historical setting. Poetry is not to be read like history; folklore can carry much meaning without being literal fact. Prophecy takes on great contemporary meaning when it is read, not as bare prediction, but as the message of judgment and hope which God spoke through his servants to a sinful, suffering people like ourselves. In biblical drama, as in any other, the main requirement is not that the characters be historical figures but that they speak and act in a way that is true to life. The same may be said of the short stories—some shorter, some longer—with which the Bible abounds. This is not to say that there is no reliable history in the Bible, for, taken as a whole, it is most of all a historical record. However, it is clearly impossible to get at the Bible's real meaning if one attempts to read its many kinds of literature as if they were all one kind.

Fourth, we must try to discover what is its timeless truth. This requires perspective by which to judge what to lay stress upon because true "yesterday, today, and forever," and what to let pass as something local, belonging only to the time when the book was written. Some parts of the Bible, like the dimensions of the tabernacle and long lists of names in the Old Testament, are outdated for us, while other parts, like the great hymns of devotion in the psalms, say for us now just what we should like to say if we could form words of such beauty and power. Most of the Bible is so much alive today that when we read it with understanding it startles us with its present-day meaning. But we cannot find its permanent truth unless we are willing to let some things pass as reflecting merely the viewpoint of an earlier day. No better phrase has been coined to describe this fact than Dr. Fosdick's statement that we find in the Bible "abiding truth in changing categories." [3]

But how are we to judge what is true if conflicts emerge? Having done all that we can to discover the historical background, literary style, and contemporary circumstances of a book or passage, we may still be left wondering what is the divine, eternal truth in it. Interpretations differ. And which is right?

Two guideposts are essential here. One is that we must do the best we can with all the knowledge available to us, and not expect our conclusions to be perfect. No human being is as wise as God, and lacking divine

[3] In his *The Modern Use of the Bible*, now an old book but an extremely useful guide to biblical interpretation.

wisdom we cannot get beyond all possibility of error in even so vital a thing as understanding the Bible. There is always room for growth as we understand it better, and much need for tolerance toward the opinions of those who differ from us.

But the second guidepost is still more essential, and this brings us to our final principle. We must interpret the lower by the higher, the Old Testament by the New, all parts of the Bible by the spirit, the words, the life of Jesus. Along with high moral insights, crude ethical concepts are to be found in the Old Testament—polygamy, slavery, stealing, deceit, psalms of vengeance[4] against enemies. This is not the mood of Jesus, and it should not be ours. Along with a great sense of dependence on God there is also a barren adherence to the letter of the law which Jesus condemned. In the Sermon on the Mount he says repeatedly, "Ye have heard that it was said to them of old time, . . . but I say unto you. . . ." In case of doubt he is our guide.

This is not to say that in the Gospels we have a record so exact that this is itself exempt from interpretation. What we have in the New Testament is a portrait reflecting the thought of the early church rather than a biography of Jesus. Nevertheless, the more one finds his way by God's leading into what Paul calls "the mind of Christ," the more this gives perspective which throws

[4] Usually called imprecatory psalms. There is an example in Psalm 137:9, "Happy shall he be, that taketh and dasheth thy little ones against the stones."

meaning on the Bible as a whole. Such knowledge of the mind of Christ is in part the result of study of the New Testament, in part the product of trying to live by its demands. It is an ever-growing appreciation of what is meant by the fact that in Jesus we see what God is and does. When we read the rest of the Bible in this light, the unimportant recedes, and the central truth of God's judgment, mercy, and saving power stands out from every page. Problems remain, but assurance of the great central certainties is the fruit of our inquiry.

## 3. Applications and examples

Thus far I have not tried to give more than passing illustrations, for to apply any of these principles effectively, we must take into account all of them. However, we must conclude by seeing what difference they make in a few of the more disputed biblical passages.

To begin with the first chapter of Genesis, no end of trouble has arisen from the fact that its six-day creation seems squarely to conflict with the findings of geology, biology, and anthropology. If the earth has been many millions of years in fashioning and man is the product of a long evolutionary development, must we not throw out either science or the Bible?

We need do neither if it is understood that the creation story was never intended as science, but as epic poetry. Whether to call it a myth depends on the meaning of the word. It is not myth as mere legend or fiction, but it is a story giving in majestic, poetic narrative an

33

early Hebrew answer to our own questions, "Who made the world?" and "Why?" It is not to be wondered at that those who retold and finally wrote the story as it was handed down did not have all the information we have about scientific processes. They were not even careful to get the sequence as straight as they might have, for day and night and the appearance of grass, herbs, and fruit trees are put before the creation of the sun! Nevertheless, what is to be marveled at is the depth of their religious insight. "In the beginning God created the heaven and the earth. . . . And God saw that it was good. . . . And God said, Let us make man in our image, after our likeness." Such words say the most sublime and the most true things that can be said about our world—that it is God's world, that it is a good world in spite of all its pain, that man in his spiritual nature is akin to divinity and has a God-given destiny. This is what the New Testament says, though in a different setting, and what an unprejudiced judgment must lead us to conclude.

To pass to the story of the Fall in the third chapter, this likewise is neither to be rejected nor taken just as it stands. It deals with the coming of evil into God's good world. As we ask, "Why?" so the early Hebrews asked it, and answered in terms of the sin of Adam and Eve. A doctrine of inherited original sin, which we do well to question, has long been held on this basis. Quite apart from the possibility of inheriting guilt, we had better assume responsiblity for our own

34

sin instead of blaming Adam! Nevertheless, there is in all of us a tendency to want to be "as gods," to run our own lives instead of letting God rule them, to use our God-given knowledge of good and evil for selfish enjoyment. Wherever this happens, we fall from what God desires of us, and God has to punish us. The truth in this story, as in the story of the Flood, the tower of Babel and many others, is that a man cannot sin against God and flout his righteous rule without bringing destruction upon himself and others.

Outside of the creation story no part of the Bible has caused more disagreement than the adventures of Jonah and the whale. But since the story is an allegory, and was never intended as literal history, the dimensions of the whale's gullet are of minor importance! What makes the story a major watershed in Old Testament literature is the often-overlooked fact of its missionary message. God sent Jonah to Nineveh far beyond the confines of Israel to preach the gospel. When he disobeyed and fled to Tarshish (Spain), God punished him, changed his course, and again sent him eastward to convert the people of Nineveh. What the book of Jonah is really trying to say to us is,

> There's a wideness in God's mercy,
> Like the wideness of the sea.

Instead of reading Daniel for mysterious prophecies about the war and other current happenings, let us read it for what it is—a great book of encouragement to faith in the midst of persecution and the collapse of earthly supports. Written during the cruel persecutions of the Jews under the madman Antiochus Epiphanes, its unknown author tells his countrymen that in spite of tyranny and anti-Semitism they can still trust and serve the God of their fathers. Lion's den or fiery furnace may engulf them; nothing can destroy them. The high point of the story, which could have come out of modern Germany, is the answer of the three Hebrew youths to the tyrant:

Our God whom we serve is able to deliver us from the burning fiery furnace; and he will deliver us out of thy hand, O king. *But if not,* be it known unto thee, O king, that we will not serve thy gods, nor worship the golden image which thou hast set up.

To cite more briefly a few instances from the New Testament, the casting out of demons can now be understood as the cure of insanity, neuroses, and accompanying physical ills by the radiant spiritual power of Christ. Paul's injunction to women to "keep silence in the churches" had meaning for his day, when only women of unsavory reputation made themselves conspicuous in public, but hardly holds for ours. The expectation of an intervention to set aside this earthly regime and usher in God's kingdom was so common in the first century of the Christian era that to overlook it is to misunderstand much of the New Testament. The symbolism used in Revelation to describe the last great conflict between Christ and Antichrist, like the beautiful imagery of the new heaven and the new earth, can hardly be taken as literal description or exact prophecy. Rather they are intimations of God's agelong struggle with evil and the assurance of his final victory. Their keynote is in the stirring words of the "Hallelujah Chorus:"

The kingdoms of this world shall become the Kingdom
     of our Lord and of His Christ,
And He shall reign forever and ever.

These are but a few of the passages on which an historical-spiritual interpretation throws much more light than does a literal dead-level reading. One must, of course, pursue such a study at length for himself to get its full significance. Read in faith and with an open-minded search for truth, the Bible yields treasure so incomparable that a lifetime is not long enough to grasp it all.

## Chapter III

## RELIGION AND SCIENCE

No DOUBT THE reader is anxious to get on to such questions as: "What is the distinctive message of Christianity?" "If there is a God, what is he?" "Why doesn't he stop the suffering in the world?" "Why doesn't he answer my prayers?"

It is natural to want to plunge into the middle of things, as I have found through a good many years of teaching religion to students, who are apt to be impatient of groundwork and wish to have all the answers at once. But in theology, as in most things, the answers depend much on the approach one takes. One must know what he is using as his basis of authority if he is to follow any clear lead toward the truth. This does not mean that the truth one finds is a matter of preference, made up to suit the fancy; but it does mean that a point of view determines the way in which one tries to relate the many complex aspects of life.

Since the two most widely held types of authority are religious faith and scientific knowledge, and since these have so often seemed to present rival claims, it will be best to devote a chapter to their relations. Much confusion, bad feeling, and dogmatic championing of *either* religion *or* science to the exclusion of the other could be avoided by an understanding of agreements and differences in their purpose and procedures.

## 1. *Agreements and differences*

In the first place, science and religion move in related, but not identical, spheres. Both have to do with "one world"; hence no sharp dividing line can be drawn to cut off either from the other's territory. But the viewpoint and purpose are different. Descriptive science, often called pure science, seeks to discover the facts in some particular field through careful observation and experiment, and to formulate as laws whatever cause-and-effect relations are discovered. Applied science builds on these discoveries to utilize and control the forces of nature, and thus to produce things or cause changes that man desires. It is the descriptive sciences, such as biology, psychology, astronomy, or physics, that one generally thinks of in comparing scientific with religious knowledge, though actually it is applied science with its great achievements in technology which now is religion's chief rival in claiming man's interest and devotion.

The scientific quest is necessarily both more impartial in viewpoint and more limited in scope than the religious outlook. The ideal of pure science is freedom from personal bias in the discovery of facts. Each particular science deals with some special branch of knowledge, often with little concern for its relations to other things or for its meaning in the whole business of living. (Hence, there is foundation for the familiar squib about the expert as one "who knows more and more about less and less.") On the other hand religion, though it regards facts as essential, is chiefly concerned with their bearing on life. It asks what things matter most and what are man's duties, sources of help, goals for living. Religion centers, not in any particular aspect of nature, but in devotion to the God who is the creator of all nature; not in any one phase of our experience, but in the endeavor to make all of life better.

To illustrate the difference, to study scientifically the physiology or psychology of emotional disturbance is not the same thing as to be spiritually concerned about the sin and tragedy of the world and seek to save it. Each approach has its place, but it is not the same place. Or to use an illustration from applied science, the production of the atomic bomb is a great scientific achievement, but the question of whether it ought to be used to destroy human beings is a moral and religious question. Though scientists, as individuals, may be and often are men of high religious and moral insight, science as such is not concerned with values and ideals, but simply with the discovery of facts and their utilization to satisfy human desires.

Second, though there is faith in both fields, it is not just the same faith. No one could be a scientist who did not have faith that some discovery of knowledge is possible, and that there are regularities about the universe for him to discover. The scientific method of testing an idea by experiment means, in a sense, trying out a faith, seeing if an insight is verified by the discovery of facts. Mme. Curie and her husband could not have discovered radium or Louis Pasteur the disease-bearing germs that he located, unless they had had faith in an idea that could be tested. Such testing requires much effort and great fidelity to the ideal of truth. When the Christian puts his faith in God and the ideals of Christ to the test of living, he, like the scientist, uses the method of "try it and see."

However, religious faith requires a venturing out into greater depths. The scientist's procedure moves in the realm of the *seen*, of things visible to critical examination, often with the help of complex mechanical instruments. Religious faith is at least in part "a conviction of things not seen." As was pointed out in the first chapter, this does not mean a leap in the dark, but it does mean an assurance of God and his relation to the world which reaches beyond what is explainable in scientific terms. Hence, religious faith calls for a type of belief and action that can go a long way with science, but can never be wholly included within it.

Scientific knowledge can reinforce religion, and the more one learns through science of the marvelous intricacy and orderliness of the world, the greater seem the works of the Creator. Dr. George Washington Carver, for example, said that in his laboratory he and the Creator worked together. As one studies the growth and adaptability of living things, whether in plant or animal life, or observes the amazing exactness of things in the physical world, one may well be convinced that this does not all happen by chance. One can have a great sense of the divine Presence as he discovers new truth about God's world. However, it is not the function of science to try to answer the deeper questions of life as to why we were created, what God requires of us, and what our destiny is. A purely scientific religion does not, and cannot, exist.

Third, there is a difference between applied science and religion in their effects on life. Both exercise much control over human welfare and happiness. However, moral ideals and values—however imperfectly lived up to—are central to the nature of religion, while they do not have a corresponding place in the mammoth structure of applied science. Technology exists primarily for utility rather than service, for giving people what they ask for rather than what they need for the enrichment of life. Even in education, medical science, and social work, which have rendered very great benefit and which come closest to putting into practice what Christianity calls for in service to persons, there is often more interest in processes than in persons. The fact that applied science can be morally neutral is largely responsible for the contrast between a vast technological civilization, which may now be destroyed by the energy it has released, and the apparently meager influence of ideals of love, good will, and reconciliation.

If we put together these differences between science

and religion, what do we get? In science, there is an earnest effort to discover truth about the way the universe is fashioned and to use such discoveries to serve human desires. The things made available by science—whether in the cure of disease, the communicating of ideas through press and movie and radio, or the whole great structure of an industrial civilization—present not only problems to be solved, but instruments by which mankind can be greatly helped. But this is no substitute for religion. It is the business of religion to furnish vision and spiritual power—to see all our problems in the light of the will of God and thus to give motive, direction, and strength for the right use of whatever knowledge or instruments science provides.

We said above that religion's chief rival now is not scientific knowledge, but the ends to which it has been put in applied science. From a practical standpoint, this overshadows all other considerations, for with the coming of the atomic bomb the very survival of man upon earth depends upon the kind of good will and world co-operation that the Christian religion stands for. When life on a large scale is carried on as if God and his moral demands did not exist, we get what D. Elton Trueblood in *The Predicament of Modern Man* has called a "cut-flower civilization"—one that has been severed from its roots. Whether Christianity can supply the roots needed for man's survival, and whether science can be used to promote "the abundant life" for all men instead of setting up rival claims, are practical issues before which the question as to whether one can believe in God and evolution seems relatively unimportant. Of this we shall have more to say in the final chapter, where the relations of Christian faith to the present social crisis will be considered.

## 2. *Types of religious belief*

The main currents of modern theology differ from each other in the attitudes held regarding the relations of science to religious truth. There are, of course, other differences, but this is a central one. It may help to understand these differences more sympathetically if we outline four main types of belief now widely held in America.

To some who have called themselves "fundamentalists," thinking the Christian fundamentals to be imperiled by modern liberal thought, science is the opponent of Christian faith wherever it seems to contradict the Bible. Though the fundamentalists first used this term about themselves to affirm the orthodoxy of their faith, it is now more often used about them to indicate a literal interpretation of the Bible and adherence to conservative views. At the opposite extreme are the naturalists who refuse—or claim to refuse—to accept any belief unless it can be scientifically tested and verified. In between are the religious liberals, sometimes called "modernists," though the latter term is not a true description because the basic principles of liberalism are very old. The liberals believe that we should

44

learn all the science possible, studying it without fear because the truth about God cannot be shaken by any truth we learn about his world; yet for answers to the deeper questions about God and the world and our place in it, religious faith is necessary. Of late there has arisen somewhat in reaction to liberalism an influential trend called the "new orthodoxy." This movement accepts the findings of science at those points where the fundamentalists think there is conflict with the Bible, but, strongly emphasizing man's sin and weakness, rejects any reliance on science or human wisdom as a source of man's salvation.

We shall not attempt in any detail to defend or to refute these positions. To examine thoroughly what each one stands for would require the writing of another book, and any brief statement will fail to do justice to some things that the exponents of these schools of thought consider important. However, since the reader is entitled to know from what point of view this book is written, I shall survey rapidly what I believe to be the main points of strength and weakness in these approaches.

Each of these positions has been championed as a protest against some error in its opposite. But there is *some* truth, as well as probably some error, in each. The first three have arisen repeatedly in the course of the centuries because they stood for something real, and the fourth is "new" only because both the historical approach to the Bible—which it accepts—and the

45

general reliance on scientific knowledge and control—which it rejects—are relatively recent developments.

The fundamentalists have been right in contending that some fundamental truths, set forth in the Bible and lying at the center of Christian faith, must be defended. In the point at which the conflict between religion and science has been most acute, the theory of evolution, those who have fought against it have believed that to accept it would be to reject the Bible, to eliminate God, and to belittle man. As we saw in the last chapter, it does not have these results if evolution is thought of, not materialistically, but as the eternal process through which the Creator works to fashion his supreme creation. The fundamentalists, though right in defending such basic elements in faith as a spiritual interpretation of God, man, and Bible, have made a mistake in refusing to look at the Bible in its historical setting. Much light is thrown upon it when one sees that the Bible contains human error as well as divine truth, and reads it for the spiritual truth that its writers in a pre-scientific age were trying to express as they wrestled with the eternal problem of creation. If one clings to a literal understanding of the Bible, it is easy to become dogmatic in defense of a traditional idea and, in opposing scientific knowledge, stand in the way of religious truth also by unnecessarily creating conflict between them.

Those at the other end who have insisted on a scientific basis for any belief have been actuated, for the most part, by a desire to get rid of all wishful thinking, all traditional baggage, all substitution of private faith for publicly provable truth. They have caught hold of one side of the important two-sided fact that for effective living both open-mindedness and conviction are necessary. Carrying open-mindedness to extremes, they have been hit by a boomerang, for when to avoid dogmatism one closes his mind to all facts that cannot be got at scientifically, the next step is dogmatically to assert that scientific knowledge is the *only* knowledge. This is, in effect, to say that the world of nature is the only world (naturalism) or at least that it is the only world we can know anything about (agnosticism, positivism). Religion, consequently, either goes by default, or becomes transformed into something other than Christian faith.[1] Humanism, the substitution of social idealism for faith in God, which was so influential a product of this movement two decades ago, has now become a very minor influence in religious circles, though something like it still dominates the thinking of great numbers of intellectually cultured persons.

Liberalism centers in a protest against dogmatism in both religion and science. It stands for the spirit of free inquiry, for confidence that with God as creator and sustainer of the world there can be no real con-

[1] The best attempt to preserve religion in naturalistic terms has been made by Henry Nelson Wieman. However, though he believes in God and is not a humanist, his God is a process of growth rather than the personal God of the main stream of Christian theology.

flict between religious and scientific truth, for the dignity of all persons as creatures of supreme worth in God's sight, for the moral challenge to work with God for the advancement of his kingdom of justice and love. These ideas are of the greatest importance, both to a grasp of the truths of Christianity and its service to human need. Yet liberalism has not been without its shortcomings. In its more extreme forms it capitulated to science almost to the point of kowtowing before it, and in emphasizing the dignity of man it gave too little recognition to the fact of human sin and the ever-present need of divine forgiveness and grace.

So the new orthodoxy came along to challenge liberalism and, as its exponents are fond of saying, to strip off its "illusions." In the approach of this position to scientific knowledge it is at one with liberalism in holding that there is no fundamental conflict. However, man's boasted confidence in the power of science to remake and cure the ills of the world comes in for strong attack. The human predicament of sin and weakness, even in the best and most Christian of persons, needs to be recognized to humble us before God and to dispel the fallacy of man's self-sufficiency. Not pride in scientific achievement or confidence in man's good will, but repentance before God is the appropriate attitude of the Christian. This note has been sounded at a time when the collapse of the social fabric of Western civilization was demonstrating the inappropriateness of human pretension and pride. It has sometimes tended to underestimate man's dignity and greatness as a child of God, and has perhaps been too pessimistic about man's capacity to work with God for the remaking of society according to Christian ideals. Nevertheless, it has been a wholesome corrective to liberalism at its weakest points and has challenged many liberals to rethink and deepen their theology.

What, then, are we to say to the relations of religion and science in the pursuit of truth? The wise Christian will make his approach both through the revelation of God in the Bible and through all that God has written in "this mysterious universe"—though the glory of God revealed supremely in the face of Jesus Christ and through sympathetic understanding of both the worth and the weakness of God's human children. Open always to more truth from whatever source it comes, suspending judgment when necessary till relative certainty emerges, resolved to live by the truth one has and to let others differ if their insights lead in another direction, one combines tolerance with decisiveness, open-mindedness with Christian conviction. Such an attitude leads both to knowledge and to power. The greatest word ever spoken about the pursuit of truth is the word of Jesus, "Ye shall know the truth. and the truth shall make you free "

## Chapter IV.

# THE REALITY AND NATURE OF GOD

*T*HERE IS MORE than one way to get at the reality and nature of God. One may go to the Bible, and supremely to the life and words of Jesus, to find God there. That is the way most Christians find him, and to many this seems all we need. Others, not wishing to depend so much on faith and revelation, prefer to approach the matter through the evidences accessible to all in nature, history, and human personality. Still a third route is the personal discovery of God through worship, through moral obedience to God's will in service, through triumphant victory over evil.

All of these routes have much to contribute to our understanding. In fact, none of them is complete without the other two. In this chapter we shall approach the matter from each of the first two angles and try to show how they illumine and supplement each other. Later when we consider the meaning of the Christian life, we shall take up the third.[1]

## 1. *The existence of God*

In the Bible the existence of God is not questioned: it is throughout assumed. Yet any inquiring mind has

---

[1] Chapters VIII and IX.

a right to raise the questions: "Why should I believe in God?" "What is the evidence?" Since the question of God's *existence* is logically prior to his *nature*, we shall begin our study with it and start with the second of the approaches outlined above.

The first reason for believing in God is the *religious experience of humanity*. The idea is one that must be lived rather than proved, and belief in God is a characteristically human experience. This is not to say that it is instinctive, that every person has it, or even that all peoples have it, for this is a matter in dispute. Rather, it is natural and normal to seek after God, and the person who does not do so is abnormal—just as it is the normal thing to be able to distinguish colors, while here and there is a person who is color-blind. There seems to be an upwelling urge in the human heart to find God—a tendency which made the French philosopher Sabatier say that man is "incurably religious." Augustine expressed this very beautifully centuries ago when he said, "Thou hast made us for Thyself, O God, and our hearts are restless until they rest in Thee."

While this religious impulse does not give positive proof of God, it affords a very strong evidence. Everywhere else in our experience where there is a powerful impulse within us, there is something outside of us responding to it. We have a hunger impulse—and there is food; a sex impulse—and there are mates; a yearning for friendship—and there are friends. The probability is great that mankind would not have a hunger for God unless there were a God to satisfy it.

But it is not alone man's impulse to worship which leads one to believe in God; it is the *kind of life* which flowers from it. Not all great souls have been Christians, but the noblest living of the ages has been rooted in religious faith. The people I know who bear suffering most bravely, who are most serene and poised in the face of difficulties, who are most sympathetic toward others, who live the most genuinely happy lives, are the people to whom faith in God is a vital reality. One of them, a lady ninety-one years old who has lost her family and her property and has almost lost her sight, has strengthened my faith repeatedly by saying with no trace of self-pity, "God never fails. When he takes away one thing, he always gives another." It is simple, triumphant faith like that which G. A. Studdert-Kennedy[2] must have had in mind when he wrote:

> Peace does not mean the end of all our striving,
> Joy does not mean the drying of our tears;
> Peace is the power that comes to souls arriving
> Up to the light where God Himself appears.

When one comes face to face with a person who carries his faith in God with him and lives by it whatever comes, doubts recede.

[2] A British clergyman and poet, chaplain to King George V. The passage quoted is from "The Suffering God," from *The Unutterable Beauty*, and is used by permission of the publishers, Harper & Bros.

Moreover, the *currents of history* give evidence of God's reality. There is a moral law written in the structure of men and nations which cannot be flouted without catastrophe. In smoother days this was not so evident. But one thing the war has demonstrated with terrible clearness is that when a society attempts to run on the basis of greed, hate, vindictiveness, and selfishness, disaster results for everybody. "God is not mocked," and what we sow we reap. The fact of evil, like the presence of goodness in the world, gives evidence of a moral order in which can be seen the governing hand of God.

Other reasons for belief in God come out of *the sciences*. Evolution gives one of the clearest possible evidences. To suppose that everything progressed from star dust to amoeba, and from amoeba to man, and from Neanderthal man to Socrates and Jesus just by accident, puts a terrific strain on our credulity. The more one learns both of biological evolution and of the evolution of social cultures, the more one sees that Tennyson was right when he said: "Yet I doubt not through the ages one increasing purpose runs."

When I consider what astronomers tell us about the magnificent distances in the skies, I find new meaning in the psalmist's words, "The heavens declare the glory of God: the firmament showeth his handiwork." When we look up into the sky at night, we not only see soft beauty; we see light that has been on its way—so distant are many of the stars—since before we were born, since before our Republic was established, since before Columbus saw America, since before Jesus lived. In fact, two thousand years, or two thousand centuries, are a short interval in cosmic time, and astronomers catch rays in their telescopes from stars many millions of light-years away. The sun and moon and planets keep going their way with such infinite accuracy that the astronomers and mathematicians can predict to the second when an eclipse will occur. To suppose that all this happens by chance is unthinkable. Wherever there is order and harmony, there is an ordering, harmonizing Mind.

When one thinks or the immensity of the universe, one is apt to feel, as a certain psalmist once did, that man is a tiny and insignificant fragment in this vastness. You remember he said:

When I consider thy heavens, the work of thy fingers,
The moon and the stars, which thou hast ordained;
What is man, that thou art mindful of him?

When I find myself in this mood, I think also of the greatness and dignity of man, and I find myself answering with the psalmist:

For thou hast made him but little lower than God,
And crownest him with glory and honor.

It appears, then, that in *the nature of human personality* there is an evidence of God. It is right to say,

"Man is an animal"; it is wrong to say, "Man is nothing but an animal." Sometimes you may yearn for a sort of bovine contentment and the easy existence of the "happy oyster," but you would not, if you could, change places with a cow or an oyster! Man's thirst for knowledge, his power to do serious thinking, his aspiration toward moral ideals, his appreciation of beauty, his quest for God—these are traits which put man above and outside of the subhuman world.

Later we shall have more to say about the Christian doctrine of man. But for the present it is enough to point out that the very fact of our existence (even with all the badness there is in us!) points beyond man's own existence and beyond the forces of physical nature for an explanation. As the old adage has it, "Water cannot rise higher than its source," and man with all his faults is still a creature of such dignity and potential goodness that he bears in him the marks of divinity. In fact, man's highest traits, the capacity for love and goodness, wisdom and creativeness, are the very traits which the Christian faith ascribes to God in infinite degree. It is reasonable to believe that mind, spirit, or personality in man emerged from lower forms of life only if a Supreme Mind, Spirit, or Personality directed the process and fashioned man according to his good purposes. This is part of what is meant by saying that God has made man in his own image.

## 2. *The nature of God*

In discussing the evidence for God's existence, we have already suggested some things about his nature. The religious strivings of mankind point to a God who gives support and makes moral demands upon us. History shows what happens when we work with, or thwart, his righteous will. Science gives evidence from which to infer the existence of a God of creative power and infinite wisdom in the fashioning of an orderly world. Man at his best, though always far from God's perfection, reveals intimations of the meaning of divinity.

We must now ask more directly what is meant by a "personal God." This term is confusing to many, for it seems to indicate a physical body, or a magnified man—often mentally pictured in childhood as a benign, elderly gentleman with a beard, seated on a throne somewhere up in heaven. When this anthropomorphic[3] conception fades as one's thinking becomes more mature, often there is nothing left.

It is necessary to decide to what extent we may, and may not, rightly think of God from what we know of human personality. Certainly if God is personal, he cannot be a superman, either with a beard and bones or a cosmic nervous system. So to think of him would

---

[3] Literally, "man-form," from the Greek *anthropos*, "man," and *morphē*, "form." Any conception of a personal God is in some respects anthropomorphic, but the danger lies in conceiving personal traits too physically and crudely.

be to make him in our image. The throne of God is picture language to suggest his majesty, and is not to be located anywhere in astronomical space. Yet this is not to deny God's personality. If the most essential thing about man is not his physical body but his spirit—the invisible *you* that dwells in and expresses your self through your body without being identical with it—so God's Spirit needs no visible, tangible body to be personal. A medium of expression he must have, just as we need our bodies, and this we find in nature, in history, in great human experiences, and supremely in God's revelation of himself in Christ. From all these sources we see in God infinite creative power and wisdom, righteousness, loving concern that seeks to lift men toward his own goodness. This is to say that God is personal, spiritual in nature as we are, but with a personality that is flawless and complete while ours at best is sin-stained and fragmentary.

From this follows a conviction very important to Christian faith and living. If God is personal, this means that we can have fellowship with him. Indeed, we can go farther and say that he has made us for fellowship with himself, and for doing his will in fellowship. This makes prayer sublimely meaningful, and imparts challenge and power to service. The personality of God is not an abstract question only; it is our final source of assurance as we seek in companionship with him to meet what life demands.

In what has been said thus far, our thought has been mainly centered in what can be discovered about God from our observation of life. Even apart from the direct witness of the Bible, the evidences of a personal God are woven into the fabric of existence. But our concept will not be complete, and is not likely greatly to transform our living, unless it is made concrete and potent in terms of what the Bible gives us.

The three dominant biblical ideas of the nature of God, converging in the New Testament to make a fourth, are of God as Creator, Judge, and Saviour. It is God who "in the beginning . . . created the heaven and the earth." The moral purpose of God is expressed in the great refrain of the creation poem, "And God saw that it was good." Though the biblical writers lived before the dawn of modern science, they caught something of the meaning of the orderly ways of God in nature and expressed it beautifully at the conclusion of a quaint old story, "While the earth remaineth, seedtime and harvest, and cold and heat, and summer and winter, and day and night shall not cease." In many passages, particularly in the psalms and in the great hymn to creation at the end of the book of Job, there are praises to God for the beauty and bounty of the world he has made. It is assumed throughout that man is dependent on, and responsible to, the God who has created him and given him "dominion over the fish of the sea, and over the fowl of the air," and over all the earth as God's steward.

In the Bible God is not only the creator—as we commonly assume—but the Judge of all men—as we tend to forget. This is not to say that a God of wrath visits vengeance upon sinners, though this all-too-human note crept into the Old Testament and has corrupted Christian theology. God as judge is a moral being who will not tolerate sin, and who seeks to save the sinful even

58

though he has to punish them to bring them to his way. An all-righteous God demands of men obedience to his his holy will. ("Shall not the Judge of all the earth do right?") Yet men persist in sin, and repeatedly in mercy God sends his messengers to save men from destruction by calling them to repentance. "Seek the Lord, and ye shall live" stands side by side with the message of judgment and doom in the words of the prophets, and gives to their indictments a positive meaning as the expression of God's mercy. The climax of the Old Testament is the foreshadowing of a Messiah, or Deliverer, to be sent from God to save the people from their sins and bring in a new age of peace and righteousness.

It is the Christian faith that in Jesus this Saviour came, and that in him we see God manifesting himself in a human life. Jesus' name for God was Father, and uniquely beyond all other men he lived as a son of God ought to live. In Jesus we have the world's supreme revelation of God. Jesus lived like God; prayed to God; triumphed over temptation and pain in Godlike mastery; gave himself like God in love and suffering for men. The cross is the eternal symbol of the union of love with suffering—of love and suffering at the heart of the universe. It is not by accident that people find the way to God most readily, not through speculation, but through devotion to the Christ in whom God has revealed himself that men may know what God is like.

If we believe in "the God and Father of our Lord Jesus Christ" not merely with intellectual assent, but with a vital and personal faith, it will do something to our living. We cannot afford to live cheaply or carelessly in the presence of such greatness.

We shall find ourselves growing daily in richness and fullness of life. We shall find our horizons broadened and our sympathies deepened. What I want to say about this has been said for me in a poem by Jessie Wiseman Gibbs:

> If we believed in God, there would be light
> Upon our pathway in the darkest night.
>
> If we believed in God, there would be power
> To foil the tempter in the sorest hour.
>
> If we believed in God, there would be peace
> In this world's warfare, ever to increase.
>
> If we believed in God, there would be joy,
> Even in tears, that nothing could destroy.
>
> If we believed in God, there would be love
> To heal all wounds and lift the world above.
>
> Lord Christ, be near us, that, beholding Thee,
> We may believe in God and be set free!

### 3. *The problem of evil*

We shall not attempt to deal here with all the questions regarding God and his relation to the world. In a sense, the whole book deals with this theme. There is, however, a persistent question that ought to have some attention in this chapter. This is the age-old problem of evil and, in particular, of unmerited suffering.

The problem of evil has two sides, sin and suffering.[4] Both raise serious questions as to the goodness and power of God, and keep us forever asking, "Why?"

Though sin is the worse evil, it presents fewer intellectual problems. If once we grant that God has endowed us by creation with enough freedom to choose between good and evil, it follows that when we thwart his will by wrong choices, we sin. The question may still be asked as to why God did not create us to be automatically good. However, I have met no one who wanted to become an automatic robot. It is God's supreme gift of freedom that makes us men. When God made us, he trusted us enough to place this dangerous gift in human hands—and took the consequences.

We shall later have more to say of sin, when we discuss the nature of man and salvation. For the present we must center on a knottier problem—why it is that good people have to suffer.

The commonest answer, both in the Old Testament and in many people's thought today, is that suffering is the punishment of God for some open or secret sin. "What have I done that God should bring this upon me?" is a frequent cry. It is true, as we saw earlier in this chapter, that there is such a thing as divine judgment, and that suffering does come to individuals and nations as a consequence of sinning against the laws of God. Nevertheless, it is not true that all suffering is to be thus explained. There are many cases of illness, be-

---

[4] My *Conflicts in Religious Thoughts*, chapters IX and X, and *The Recovery of Ideals*, chapter XIII, give a fuller treatment than is possible here. See also *The Dark Night of the Soul* for a discussion of the convergence of sin and suffering in mental depression.

reavement, and tragic loss which are not to be traced to the sufferer's sin. The book of Job was written to refute the idea that all suffering comes from sin, and the sooner this idea is abandoned, the better.

How, then, are we to explain it? No human mind is wise enough to give a complete answer, but three important facts give us a clue. The first is our freedom. Not all, but much, of the world's misery is caused by human ignorance, folly, and sin. The second is a world of regularity and order in which causes bring effects. The third is the fact that we live in a great network of social relations—so bound together that my good helps another, and my evil harms another. These factors—freedom, order, and society—are our greatest blessings, without which we should be miserable, if indeed we could live at all. Yet they sometimes cause suffering. This can only mean that, for the sake of the goodness of this kind of world, God permits some things to happen that he does not desire, and suffers with us in our pain.

This may become clearer if we let the reader ask some questions. By this time he is saying: "You speak of God's goodness. What about his power? If he could have prevented the war, why didn't he?"

God's omnipotence is important. There is not merely a prop to bolster our courage, but an authentic Christian conviction in "Hallelujah! for the Lord God omnipotent reigneth!" This confidence must not be surrendered. It can be preserved by the faith that God's victory is sure.

But does this mean literally that "with God all things are possible"? If we try to say so, it lands us in contradictions. In the nature of things, he could not make a square triangle or a yardstick a foot long. And some limits are imposed by his own nature. If he is perfect in goodness, he cannot be sinful; if he is all-wise, he cannot be foolish and erratic. When he acts, he must act consistently.

In making men with moral freedom God has greatly limited his own freedom. In order to choose to obey his will, we must be free to thwart it. If to avert war God took from us our power to sin, he would be treating us as puppets instead of persons. He would, furthermore, be acting, not like the righteous and loving Father that he is, but like a dictator.

"This I understand," the reader may be saying, perhaps a bit impatiently. "It is clear enough that we are free to sin and make mistakes, and that this causes suffering. But, is there not a great deal of suffering that cannot be attributed to human agency—such things as hurricanes, floods, earthquakes, unavoidable accidents?"

Yes. There are some things we can neither predict nor prevent. The key both to understanding these events and to preventing some of them is the fact that God works through orderly natural processes. We do not know all of his ways, but many of them have been discovered and formulated as "laws of nature." We have some knowledge of them.

These regularities are a great blessing to us. We depend on them not only for our scientific knowledge but for our security in daily living. Imagine—if you can—the resulting chaos if gravitation were for a moment interrupted! Or, if fire were withdrawn, which the Greeks said Prometheus stole from the gods for man's benefit. But if God is to work through orderly processes, these processes must go on even when great suffering results.

God cannot at the same time give us gravitation and fire as dependable forces and suspend them when an incendiary bomb drops from the sky to wreak devastation on what lies under it.

"This brings us to the heart of the problem for me!" the reader may exclaim. "That bomb killed innocent civilians who had little, if anything, to do with causing the war. How can a just God let this happen?"

If this were all, it would be grossly unjust. We are all sinners before God, but some have far greater guilt than others. Often the relatively innocent suffer most.

However, from the Christian point of view light is thrown on what would otherwise be stark mystery. We live in the family of God. So knit together are we that we inevitably gain by another's good and lose by another's evil. This causes tragic suffering of the innocent. But it challenges us to work with God to make this family relation one from which all can profit. It is our ground of hope for the advancement of God's Kingdom. It puts before us the continuing Christian obligation to banish suffering by means of self-giving love.

When suffering is voluntarily assumed by the innocent for the guilty, this is the way of the cross. It lies at the heart of the Christian faith. But the cross would be meaningless for us if God did not suffer too. "He that spared not his own Son, but delivered him up for us all"—have not these words taken on deeper meaning as parents have been called to give sons in our time? Whatever happens to men, God suffers most.

Our little minds have not penetrated the whole mystery. To do so we should have to be as wise as God, and we are not. But the last word in the problem of pain is not understanding of the mystery, but mastery. With the living companionship of God, whose love for the world is equaled only by his agony for human sin and pain, any suffering can be endured. More than that, it can be made a channel for the lifting of life nearer to God's presence. Hosts of victorious lives, triumphant in the midst of pain, bear witness. If we will let God work in us to refine, sweeten, and glorify our living, then we shall discover the meaning of Paul's words: "We know that the whole creation has been groaning in travail together until now; . . . we know that in everything God works for good with those who love him." [5]

It is through spiritual victory over pain and the turning of it to his good ends, not by any assurance of its removal, that God delivers us from the evil of suffering. This is central to the Christian gospel. We must next ask what there is about the Christian's faith in Jesus Christ that gives us grounds of hope.

[5] Romans 8:22, 28 (Revised Standard Version).

# Chapter V

## JESUS CHRIST OUR LORD

*S*INCE INFANCY most of us have heard or uttered prayers which ended, "Through Jesus Christ our Lord." Since the beginning of Christianity Christians have called Jesus "Lord," and have in some way equated him with God. What does this mean?

In the preceding chapter we saw that our surest clue to the reality and nature of God is in Jesus, and that through this conviction, if earnestly held and lived by, new power flows into our lives. This is to say that in Jesus the Christian sees the Revealer of God and the Redeemer of men. We must now ask further what these terms—and others related to them—mean for us.

### 1. *Jesus the Revealer*

Jesus is not our only avenue to the discovery of God. As we have seen, in the beauty and bounty and orderliness of nature, in the best of human insights and strivings of the ages, in the upward climb of man and even in the thwarting of human desire that abruptly halts our course when we sin against God, are revelations of the Eternal. But gleaming high above all is the manifestation of God in human life that Jesus Christ presents. When we see Jesus, we know what God is and what he requires of us.

The Christian doctrine of the "incarnation" means that in Jesus we see God "in the flesh," or, as the Fourth

Gospel puts it in immortal words: "The Word was made flesh, and dwelt among us, (and we beheld his glory, the glory as of the only begotten of the Father,) full of grace and truth." [1] Paul says almost the same thing when he writes in his second letter to the Corinthians: "For God, who commanded the light to shine out of darkness, hath shined in our hearts, to give the light of the knowledge of the glory of God in the face of Jesus Christ." [2]

When we ask what this light of God's glory is that we see in the face of Jesus, we must do what the first disciples did—get acquainted with him. And the more we read the story and let the mysterious radiance and beauty, the gentleness and valiant strength, of his personality capture us, the more plausible it appears to say that the glory of God shines in his face. We do not have in the Gospels a biography of Jesus, but a portrait drawn by the first-century Christians. After due allowances are made for their interpretations written into the story, the outlines still are unmistakable; and a clear, luminous figure shines through the dust upon the portrait to show us God.

Read one of the Gospels through at a sitting, and see what it says to you. The best Gospel for this purpose is Mark's—the earliest and most dependable account of Jesus' life. However, Matthew contains the epitome of his teachings in the Sermon on the Mount.

It is apparent that here is a man who had a remarkable power over people, and that this power was joined to

[1] John 1:14.
[2] II Corinthians 4:6.

67

sympathy with and concern for everybody. He was never too busy to heal and help the multitudes of people who needed him. Others might give a wide berth to lepers and poor insane folk thought to be possessed of devils, but not he. Other "respectable" people condemned him for eating and chatting with tax-gatherers and sinners, but he saw that they too had souls that needed help. He had time to play with children and to talk with women—two things common enough now as a result of centuries of Christian influence, but not then. When a Roman centurion's son or a Syrophoenician woman's daughter needed help, he broke across racial lines to give it; and one of his greatest parables is of the neighborly act of a despised Samaritan. Wherever he went, he healed the sick, encouraged the fearful, gave new life to the weak and the sinful whose faith reached out to him for deliverance. He did for men, in outgoing, inclusive love for all, what in our best insights we know God is seeking to do for us. In such acts of Jesus we see the glory of the Father, "full of grace and truth."

In the words of Jesus that we have recorded there is no high-flown rhetoric. He taught mainly by simple stories about things familiar to his hearers—the sower and his seed, the shepherd and his sheep, a woman sweeping her house for a lost coin, a boy leaving his father's house to have his fling and coming back home again poorer but wiser, mustard seed growing to make a great tree, leaven making the bread rise, birds, lilies, wineskins, fishing nets, red sunsets, a dead sparrow along the highway, a wedding party for which the lamps must be kept bright by care and watchfulness. Whatever Jesus touched he glorified. In his and the Father's world there was nothing small or cheap. Through such homely things of everyday life he set forth the greatest truths ever spoken about God's seeking, forgiving love; about God's rule in human lives; about what God asks of those who would work with him to make his Kingdom come.

Though Jesus was not a systematic theologian and his teachings do not come neatly arranged in logical order, it is not difficult to sift from his words the primary things that he taught. About God he taught that, like a father, God loves all men and is concerned that all his sons live in good will and brotherhood with one another. About man he taught that we are weak and sinful at best, ever prone to sin against God and our neighbor, but nevertheless creatures of supreme worth and dignity in God's sight. About the nature of the good life, he taught that the greatest virtues are not those of outward obedience to the law but those of inner purity of motive, and that a life of sincerity, humility, mercy, and forgiveness is the blessed life. Regarding the things to be prized, he counseled simplicity and the placing of spiritual above material possessions. Regarding the sources of power for our salvation, he taught that through faith in God, not through any merit of our own, our broken lives can be made whole.

Regarding our destiny he spoke few words, but great comforting ones, that promise eternal life. As his central message, many times repeated, he placed before men the great ideal of the righteous rule of God in human lives, the coming of God's Kingdom on earth as it is in heaven.

When we put together what Jesus did and what he

said, we have a clue to understanding what is meant by Jesus Christ as the supreme revelation of God. At three points this stands out.

First, Jesus practiced what he preached. In all the rest of us there is a gap somewhere between what we profess and what we do. In him the fabric of his life is a seamless robe.

Second, his religion and ethics, like his life and his words, are all of one piece. This is to say that in him the worship of God, new life through God, obedience to God and to God's demands, all fit together in one inseparable whole. Wherever men have tried, even haltingly, to be followers of Jesus, they have found themselves challenged at one and the same time to love God and their fellow men. Of the two Great Commandments, neither can spare the other.

Third, Jesus had a sure, unerring sense of what was important. He took the best in the Old Testament, often marginal there, and lifted it to a place of central importance. In whatever human situation he touched, he saw to the heart of the issue and brought out new insights, latent powers, clearer direction for living. He gave no precise rules or codes of conduct, but by his discernment of what God puts first, he has been enabling men ever since to "seek . . . first the kingdom of God, and his righteousness."

If Jesus had done no more than to show men by example and precept what God is like, we would rank him first among all men. As we live with his personality and see it in all its purity and power, we too are led to say with the Roman centurion who stood by at his death, "Truly this man was the Son of God." This we must say at the very least, that Jesus was so like God that in him we behold the glory of the Father.

This is Jesus the Revealer, the incarnate Son of God. But can we say more? We must ask now what it means to say, "Jesus saves."

## 2. *Christ the Redeemer*

The word "redemption" sounds old-fashioned and meaningless to many people. It means literally to be "bought back," and came into use originally from the idea that a person who had become a slave to sin could be restored to freedom only when a price was paid. In spite of the outmoded metaphor, there is a deep meaning here, for the Christian believes that Jesus in love for men did something for us which we could not do for ourselves. However, we shall understand it better if we change the word a little and say that Christ has "brought" us back to God. Redemption means salvation, and salvation means healing, health, wholeness of living. To say that "Jesus saves" is to say that when we have strayed from our true home in God, when our souls are sick and at loose ends, he brings us back and heals and unifies us for strong and victorious living.

How does this happen? No better account has ever been given than in Jesus' own story of the prodigal son— the boy who, wishing to enjoy himself and have his own way, left home only to become very unhappy when he got his own way. "When he came to himself, he said, . . . I will arise and go to my father"; and, returning, he found salvation, for in spite of his badness his father had not ceased to love him. This is a parable that applies to us, and to human nature in every age. Not that we must

71

literally come *back* to God, for in our self-seeking we have never been really at home with him. Nor for most of us do our sins take the form of drunkenness and riotous living! What the story means is that when we try to run our own lives and have what we want, however well we may meet the requirements of ordinary decency, we fall a long way short both of the goodness and of the inner satisfaction that come from being in fellowship with God. Only as we stop trying to depend on our own merits and·"with hearty repentance and true faith" turn to God, can his forgiving mercy receive us and give to us his strength and joy.

This is what has been happening all through the centuries by the power of Christ. One thinks of Mary Magdalene, out of whom "seven devils" were driven; of Saul of Tarsus, persecuting the Christians till God blinded him on the Damascus Road to open his eyes; of Augustine, wrestling futilely with sexual temptation until God said to him, "Put ye on the Lord Jesus Christ, and make not provision for the flesh to fulfill the lusts thereof"; of Francis of Assisi, renouncing his father's wealth to serve the poor in utter simplicity and humility; of George Fox, cured of the depression that was ruining his life when he heard a voice which said, "There is One, even Jesus Christ that can speak to thy condition"; of John Wesley, having his heart "strangely warmed" until he was empowered to revitalize the faith of many thousands. As one thinks of such famous Christians, one must not forget to be grateful for the millions of humble, nameless ordinary folks of all ages and all lands who have mastered overwhelming difficulties to live greatly through the power of Christ.

72

At this point a question may arise. Is it by the power of Christ that such great living comes about? Or by the power of God? In other words, does Jesus save, or does God save us?

The answer for the Christian is *both*. It is "God in Christ" that brings about the miracle of changed lives in Christian redemption. A large part of what we mean by the divinity of Christ is involved in the fact that in Jesus' time he, like God, could forgive sins without its seeming blasphemous to the forgiven. In our time we can say either that Christ saves us or that God saves us, for it is the God who has not only *revealed* himself but *imparted* himself to us in Christ that is our salvation.

There can be only one supreme center of loyalty. That center for the Christian is not God alone, or Christ alone. It is the God who has given himself to men in Christ. It is this God, incarnate in Christ the Saviour, who of his overflowing mercy breaks the power of sin and death to deliver us from evil.

## 3. *The doctrine of the Trinity*

This gives us our clue to the understanding of the Trinity of Father, Son, and Holy Spirit. This doctrine, which emerged during the early centuries of Christian thought and is deeply imbedded in our tradition, is a puzzle to many minds. The Trinity does not mean that Christians are expected to worship three separate gods. Nor does it mean that in some peculiar manner three different persons are one person. It means, in its simplest terms, that God has expressed or manifested himself in three ways. We see something of God's nature in

73

his creating and sustaining work as Father; we see him within the conditions of human life as Son; we experience his presence within our lives as Holy Spirit.

The problem of the Trinity does not center mainly in the third element, for it is not difficult to conceive of the Holy Spirit as the indwelling presence of God in our lives. All true worship, all fellowship with God in prayer, all sense of direction from God in the daily decisions we must make, presupposes the presence of the Holy Spirit. There is a large problem as to how to distinguish between our own mistaken ideas and the true guidance God gives us through his Holy Spirit, and of this we shall say more later when we consider how to discover the will of God.[3] However, there is no serious problem in thinking that, as we open our lives to him, God manifests himself to us through the Holy Spirit.

The main question about the doctrine of the Trinity lies in what we mean by Christ. If one believes what has been said earlier in this chapter about Jesus Christ as the supreme revelation of God and the Saviour of men, he will affirm belief in Christ as the Son of God. This does not mean that Jesus *was* God. It means that his life was so filled with the character and power of God that when men have seen him, they have seen the Father.

To believe in Jesus Christ as the Son of God is the cornerstone on which Christian faith rests. In the gospel story it is recorded that when Jesus at Caesarea Philippi asked the disciples the question, "Whom say ye that I am?" Peter answered, "Thou art the Christ, the Son of

[3] Chapter XI, section 3.

the living God." [4] It was on this conviction that the Church was founded, and it is from this faith that the Church has continued to draw its power.

If we hold to this faith, a good many questions either receive an answer or assume relative unimportance. For example, the pre-existence of Christ does not mean that Jesus as a human being lived before Jesus was born. Rather, it means that the divinity in him is as eternal as God. Before Jesus came into the world, this divinity which became incarnate in him was already in the world as the eternal Creative Spirit which John's Gospel, borrowing from Greek thought, calls the "Word." [5] This same divinity remained in the world after Jesus' death to be the Comforter[6]—the Holy Spirit of God which is at the same time the Spirit of Christ.

The question as to whether Jesus was born of a virgin is one on which the opinion of Christians differ, and the biblical accounts do not throw clear light upon it. In the first chapters of Matthew and Luke a virgin birth is stated.[7] However, in both Matthew and Luke the genealogy which traces Jesus' ancestry back to King David is through Joseph's line. Jesus seems generally to have been regarded in Nazareth as Joseph's son.[8] The letters of Paul and the Gospel of John, which

[4] Matthew 16:15, 16.

[5] In Greek, the *Logos*. There is no word in English that exactly translates it. It means the eternal self-expression and outpouring of God's life into the world.

[6] John 14:26. The Revised Standard Version of the New Testament translates this more meaningfully as the "Counselor."

[7] Matthew 1:18-25; Luke 1:26-35.

[8] See Matthew 13:55; Luke 4:22. Also Luke 2:41, 48.

75

throughout affirm the divinity of Christ, make no mention of a virgin birth. It does not appear in Mark, the earliest Gospel. These facts lend support to the view that the story of a physical miracle in connection with Jesus' birth is part of the tradition that developed after the early Christians had for other reasons become convinced of his divinity.

In any case Jesus' sonship hinges, not on the physical manner of his birth, but on what he was and said and did. His life, his teachings, his power to transform lives in his own time and ever since, are evidence enough that in a unique sense he was the Son of God. Seeing in him this supreme expression of the life of God, Christians through the centuries have called him "Lord."

The whole great story—the birth, the life, the teachings, the death, the resurrection of Christ—drives us to action in Christ's name. A "lord," in the language of an earlier society, is one to whom allegiance is owed, one to whom service is due. If Jesus Christ is "Lord," not in name only, but as the Living Center of our lives, to him we shall give our supreme allegiance and our service. Out of the daily round of Christian duties, made rich by daily fellowship with Christ, comes the beginning of eternity in time. Our highest reward is no earthly blessing, but the voice of one saying, "Well done, thou good and faithful servant: thou hast been faithful over a few things, I will make thee ruler over many things: enter thou into the joy of thy Lord."

## Chapter VI

## GOOD FRIDAY AND EASTER

*T*HE LIFE OF Jesus gives us a supreme center of loyalty. In it we see God, and by its power we are lifted. But it lies at the center of Christian belief that Christ *died* for our sins. What, then, is the special place of Christ's death in our salvation?

### 1. *The meaning of the Cross*

It is not by accident that the cross is the central symbol of the Christian religion. So familiar is it that we tend to make of it merely an ornament. But without what the cross stands for, the Christian religion would neither have come into existence nor have lasted through the centuries to be today a beacon of light in a darkened world.

What the cross symbolizes is God's way of dealing with men. As the flag of our country means, not just red, white, and blue cloth in a certain pattern, but a great ideal of freedom and democracy to which we owe patriotic devotion, so the cross is not simply two crossed bars of wood or a glittering bit of gold in a vertical-horizontal position. The cross means the meeting point of suffering with love, and God's way of conquering evil through suffering love.

If we ask how the cross came to mean this union of suffering with love as God's way of delivering us from

77

evil, we are taken back to what Jesus was and what he did. That the cross is our symbol because Jesus died on the cross is obvious. But just how did his death make it our pattern and our source of power?

This question is not easy to answer, for into the saving death of Christ are compressed the mystery and miracle of God's saving love. To grasp it fully we should need, as Paul said, to "understand all mysteries," and instead of trying to make it appear entirely reasonable we had better say gratefully as Paul did, "Thanks be to God for his unspeakable gift."

Yet this does not mean that we should refuse to think. Christians at various times have had a number of doctrines of the *atonement,* that is, of the way in which Christ's death makes possible the forgiveness of sins and our "at-one-ment" with God. In spite of very unsatisfactory elements in some of them, all have some truth, and some of them great truth. Let us take a glance at them.

There is the *propitiation* theory, centering in words we still use in the Communion service: "If any man sin, we have an Advocate with the Father, Jesus Christ the righteous: and he is the propitiation for our sins; and not for ours only, but also for the whole world.' [1] When this is taken to mean, as it too often has been, that an angry God has to be appeased, the modern Christian rightly rebels. It sounds like primitive religion, and clearly is not the kind of God that Jesus worshiped and served! Jesus' God of fatherly love for all men, even sinners, needs no sin offering to propitiate his wrath.

[1] I John 2:1-2.

However, if we take the sentence before and the one after as they appear in the First Epistle of John, the meaning becomes much clearer. It reads:

My little children, these things write I unto you that ye may not sin.

And if any man sin, we have an Advocate with the Father, Jesus Christ the righteous: and he is the propitiation for our sins; and not for ours only, but also for the whole world.

And hereby we know that we know him, if we keep his commandments.

When these verses are put together, what they say is: "God desires us not to sin. Jesus is our helper to find God, and the whole world's. Our faith is proved by the way we keep his commandments." At the heart of any true doctrine of the cross or the atonement lies this ethical emphasis. Furthermore, if the term "propitiation" be translated "expiation" as it is in the Revised Standard Version of the New Testament, the emphasis then falls, not on God's anger, but on the evident fact of our sin and the need to have its burden lifted if we are to keep God's commandments.

Another doctrine, as unsatisfactory as the propitiation theory when taken in its crude form but with a kernel of true meaning in it, is the *ransom* theory. The assumption beneath it is that mankind was in the clutches of the devil until God through Christ paid the ransom in our behalf in order to release us. In support of it one finds in the Bible such passages as Paul's, "Ye were bought

79

with a price," [2] and the words attributed to Jesus, "For the Son of man also came not to be ministered unto, but to minister, and to give his life a ransom for many." [3] However, to suppose that the devil had to be "bought off" is not in keeping with the idea of salvation from sin through the power of God that one finds elsewhere in the words of Jesus and Paul! Paul's main emphasis is not that Christ appeased, but that he vanquished, the powers of evil. The truth in the ransom theory is not that sin can be canceled by another person's paying the bill; it lies rather in the fact that in his death Jesus demonstrated to the uttermost and for all time what it means "not to be ministered unto, but to minister."

A related view, though from the imagery of the law court, is the *penal satisfaction* theory. Here man the sinner is represented as incurring a penalty from God the judge—a penalty which must be paid if divine justice is to be upheld. Yet man has no good works by which to settle the score. Christ by his death takes the punishment, makes amends for our sin, purchases by his blood our forgiveness. Because of the emphasis on what Christ did in assuming the penalty of our guilt, this view is often called also the *substitutionary* theory. [4] It was formulated in classic form in the eleventh century by Anselm, archbishop of Canterbury, and has had great influence on both Roman Catholic and Protestant

[2] I Corinthians 6:20; 7:23.
[3] Mark 10:45.
[4] It is also sometimes called the "scapegoat theory." In the Old Testament the scapegoat was the goat over whose head the high priest confessed the sins of the people on the day of atonement, after which it was driven into the wilderness. See Leviticus, chapter 16.

thought. As Anselm propounded it, man's sin before God is a debt so great that no mere man, but only the God-man, could pay it; and he could make atonement, not by any act of duty that was required of him, but only by something not required—the giving of his life. Not many of us now can thus think of sin as a legal debt to be paid to God, whether by ourselves or by Christ. However, at the heart of it lies the insight that we do not earn our salvation by our own good works, but that Christ in love has done for us what we could not do for ourselves.

It is apparent by now that these theories, though they differ in imagery and emphasis, tend to merge into one another. At the root of them is the idea that the blood of Christ atones for our sin and lifts its curse. What are we to do with them?

We can reject these various doctrines of a blood atonement for their artificiality, for sin is certainly not like a money transaction which can be paid by someone else, whether to God or the devil. We can veer away from them because they suggest a vengeful, arbitrary God. At the opposite extreme, we can cling to them tenaciously, condemn those who disagree, and make of "the blood" something of almost magical potency. Or we can try to understand them, let go some elements, and retain others that seem to us profoundly true.

The last is what we ought to do. But first let us look at a theory which moves along a quite different track.

A doctrine which has appeared occasionally throughout the history of Christian thought, and which appeals to many people today, is the *moral influence* theory. It emphasizes the fact that Jesus, by his obedience to God and his fidelity to God's call even when it took him to his death, set a perfect pattern for our lives. When we look at him, we see how a completely Godlike life is lived, and by this vision we are challenged to bear our crosses and walk in his steps.

This is simpler and easier to grasp than the other theories. It has the great values of linking Jesus' death with his entire life, of sending us to the Gospels to find direction for imitating him, and of putting the central emphasis on trying to live like Christ. It corrects the mistakes of finding something magical in his death and of making salvation merely an emotional experience unrelated to Jesus' way of life. Whatever our view, these values must be retained.

Does this say all that is needed? Certainly Jesus should be our pattern. But can we live up to this pattern simply by looking at it? If he is a "moral influence" only, not victory over sin but discouragement at utter failure to live like Jesus is often the result.

The great drawback in the moral influence theory is that it "pulls the teeth" out of a central Christian conviction. For if Jesus died simply out of fidelity to his convictions when evil men misunderstood and persecuted him, wherein did his death differ from that of Socrates at the hands of the Athenians? Or of any other great, good man who died a martyr to his cause? We admire Socrates, and his influence still lives; but there is no religion that makes him the center of loyalty. The cross is on millions of church spires and altars, but I know of no corresponding symbolic use of the cup from which Socrates drank the hemlock.

We are driven, then, to look deeper for the meaning

of the cross and a doctrine of the atoning—it is clearer to say "saving"—death of Christ. The view that is truest may be called the *redemptive* or *evangelical* doctrine if one wants a name, though it has been held throughout Christian history and usually without a label.

This view centers both in the incarnation and in human experience. It takes radically the belief that "God was in Christ reconciling the world unto himself," and that in Christ we not only see the nature but find the power of God for our salvation. This God-man, sent by God to save us from our sins, could have refused his mission; but he accepted it and carried it through. He "became subject unto death, even the death on the cross, for our redemption." This means that he lived for men and died for men in suffering love as God eternally gives himself for us.

What happened on the first Good Friday is what always happens when evil men thwart God's will—the innocent suffer. But the heart of Good Friday does not lie simply in Jesus' being an innocent victim of other men's sin and blindness. Thousands have had to endure as cruel physical suffering during the war. When Jesus died, God gave himself—freely, fully, to the uttermost in love of men. The meaning of what God is *always* doing for us is focused there, and into that climactic moment in history are compressed both the pattern and the power of God's eternal work with men.

All that this means cannot be stated in an explanatory sentence or paragraph. The cross stands as our perfect pattern of suffering love; as the symbol of God's eternal self-giving for undeserving men; as the focal point in history when Divine Love met and conquered human sin. But when we have said this, for the richer overtones of meaning we still have to fall back on the words of the Bible. Those who have felt themselves lifted and brought to newness of life through Christ can find great meaning in, "God commendeth his love toward us, in that, while we were yet sinners, Christ died for us," or, "God so loved the world, that he gave his only begotten Son." To others the cross is apt to seem, as it did to the Greeks and the Jews of whom Paul spoke, "foolishness" and a "stumblingblock."

Of the many attempts outside the Bible to say what the cross means, I have found none better than that in Borden P. Bowne's *Studies in Christianity:*

I know something of the arguments whereby we seek to keep our faith in the divine goodness in the presence of the world's pain and sorrow and the manifold sinister aspects of existence. I do not disparage them; upon occasion I use them; but I always feel that at best they are only palliatives and leave the great depths of the problem untouched. There is only one argument that touches the bottom, and that is Paul's question: "He that spared not his own Son, but delivered him up for us all, how shall he not with him also freely give us all things?" We look on the woes of the world. We hear the whole creation, to use Paul's language, groaning and laboring in pain. We see a few good men vainly striving to help the world into life and light; and in our sense of the awful magnitude of the problem and of our inability to do much, we cry out: "Where's God? How can he bear this? Why doesn't he do something?" And there is but one answer that satisfies: and that is the Incarnation and the Cross. God could not bear it. He has done something.

He has done the utmost compatible with moral wisdom. He has entered into the fellowship of our suffering and misery and at infinite cost has taken the world upon his heart that he might raise it to himself.[5]

What this means for us is that there is a Cross (with a capital C) which shows us God's way as clearly as human eye can see it; a Cross on which the purest of all men suffers with, and for, guilty men like ourselves; a Cross from which comes assurance of God's forgiving love as we seek to do his commandments. From this Cross, as we make it the center of faith and loyalty, comes new power for living. What we must do then is "to take up our cross daily"—our little crosses that seem so petty by comparison—and out of them by God's strength make a Christ-centered, loving, and victorious life.

## 2. *The Resurrection*

Good Friday is the most solemn, soul-searching day in the Christian year. It should stir us to penitence; gratitude to God for his supreme, unspeakable gift; new resolution to seek to do his will. But Good Friday is not the end of the story. Around the world we sing on Easter morning:

> Christ the Lord is risen today,
> *Alleluia! Alleluia!*

Easter in our time has become largely a pagan festival. To make of it a time of feasting and new clothes is ex-

[5] P. 99, Used by permission of the publishers, Houghton Mifflin Co.

actly opposite to the spirit of One who said, "Take no thought, saying, What shall we eat? or, What shall we drink? or, Wherewithal shall we be clothed?" What it meant to the first Christians was life, power, hope, victory. It ought to mean that to us.

We cannot be sure of the details of what happened the first Easter morning. The accounts of the Resurrection differ, but the central fact is certain. To the disciples—a discouraged, disheartened little company about to go back to their fishing nets—there came the certainty that their Leader was not dead but present with them. There is infinite pathos in the word, "We hoped that it was he who should redeem Israel." [6] There is supreme rejoicing in Mary's, "I have seen the Lord"; in the testimony after the journey to Emmaus, "Did not our heart burn within us, while he talked with us by the way . . . ?"; in the "Peace be unto you," which came as the voice of hope to the gathering of troubled, questioning disciples.[7] From that time on they were no longer beaten but victorious. The little company of twelve became one hundred and twenty; and after Peter's great sermon on Pentecost three thousand souls were added in one day. Peter's text was the Resurrection, and in "the power of his resurrection" he and Paul and the other early Christians became flaming witnesses for Christ. Assured that the living Christ was with them and could carry them through any difficulty, a despised minority withstood opposition and martyrdom until their faith became that of the Roman Empire and the

[6] Luke 24:21.
[7] John 20:18; Luke 24:32, 36.

Western world. We are the inheritors of that faith, which in our time has now been carried by Christian missions around the world.

What does the Resurrection mean? It means, first, the continuity of the Jesus of history with the Christ of living faith. Though we need not be fussy about diction, we ought in strict accuracy to refer to the man of Nazareth and Jerusalem as "Jesus," and reserve the term "Christ" for the deathless divine Spirit that makes him our eternal Saviour. "Christ" means "the anointed one," the divine deliverer for whom the Jews were looking, and who came—though not as they expected—to deliver all men from evil. The Incarnation, the Cross, and the Resurrection have to be brought together until we see them as *one* divine act within history for the salvation of the world.

The living Christ is not another God, but the same God who is with us always as loving Father and indwelling Holy Spirit. The risen Christ may have appeared to the first disciples in some more tangible form than he comes to us. That is a possibility on which we can have opinions, but not certainty. What we can be certain of is that he brings to us through the Spirit of God the same victory he brought to them. This is bedrock for the Christian. Without it faith turns flabby, and our action loses verve.

This brings us to a second profound meaning of the Resurrection, Christ's conquest of sin and death. This does not mean, of course, that with the Resurrection sin and death disappeared from the earth. They are with us as man's agelong evils, and have mounted to colossal proportions in our day. What it does mean is that through the power of God they need not defeat us. Ever since the first Good Friday and Easter morning Christians have known that evil is doomed, that whatever the worst that men may do, God cannot be vanquished. This is what we mean when we sing:

> In the cross of Christ I glory,
> Towering o'er the wrecks of time.

The wrecks of time are all around us. But for the Christian this means that for every Good Friday there can be an Easter morning; that beyond tragedy lies the possibility of triumph; that where God is, no defeat— not even death—is final.

We rightly emphasize the message of Easter as the hope of God's gift of eternal life.[8] Though the immortality of the soul did not begin with Christ's resurrection, his conquest of the grave puts deep and abiding meaning into the faith that, whether in life or death, our souls are in God's keeping. "Because I live, ye shall live also" is a promise that never wears out. For ourselves and our loved ones this ought to mean, not comfort only, but the power to live, while life lasts, with courage and hope.

## 3. *The Lord's Supper*

We shall not attempt to discuss at length the meaning and authority of the sacraments. There is no point on which Christians differ more. However, since the Lord's

---

[8] See chapter X for a more extended discussion of the meaning of eternal life.

Supper has always been related to the Cross and the Resurrection, it is appropriate to note what this connection is.

The various names for it suggest the connection. Paul called it "the Lord's supper," [9] and it has been called this ever since. It commemorates the Last Supper, the time when Jesus ate the Passover feast with his disciples the night before his Crucifixion. In the early Church, before the ceremonial rite had developed, the followers of Christ met to have a meal together in memory of this event. They called it the *agape,* "love-feast," a term which suggests the warmth of their fellowship in Christ. Much of the same idea is suggested by our present word "Communion." To speak of "Holy Communion" is to recognize its sacredness. It is also called the "Eucharist," which means thanksgiving, from the thanks which Jesus expressed when he took the bread and the cup in the Last Supper. In the Catholic Church it is called the Mass, from the words in Latin at the beginning of the service (*Ite, missa est*) by which members of the congregation not qualified to take Communion are dismissed.

What ought the Communion service to mean to us? In the first place, it should bring to memory, not only the Last Supper of Jesus with his disciples, but the whole great story of his suffering, death, and resurrection for our sakes. "This is my body, which is given for you; do this in remembrance of me. . . . This is my blood of the new covenant which is shed for you, and for many, for the remission of sins"—these great and

[9] I Corinthians 11:20 ff.

89

moving words cannot be taken by Protestants to mean that by a physical miracle the bread and wine have become the actual body and blood of Christ. Nevertheless, they ought to make us think of a supremely important fact—that Jesus Christ in love gave himself for our salvation. To miss this is to miss what lies at the heart of the Christian religion.

Though the Communion is a service of commemoration, it is more than a mere reminder. Symbolically, through the use of words and forms that have varied but little through the centuries, the drama of Christ's death and the assurance of his loving presence are re-enacted. Though there can be no literal repeating of Christ's sacrifice—that was done once and for all time—its meaning for those whose lives have been quickened by it must ever be renewed. Through confession the need of salvation is declared. Through comforting words of assurance its possibility is affirmed. By it we are called "to lead a new life, following the commandments of God and walking from henceforth in His holy ways." Through the bread and wine and symbolic acts, the death of Christ ceases to be merely past history and becomes a present, saving power in the lives of the worshipers.

Another note which, we saw, inheres in the very use of the term "Communion" is fellowship. The Communion service is never a solitary act. It requires the presence at least of the minister or priest and the communicant, and usually it is celebrated in a congregation. To come to the Lord's table we ought to be "in love and charity with [our] neighbors." The act of partaking together of bread and wine in Christ's name ought to give us a sense of being in fellowship, not only with our immediate neighbors, but with our fellow Christians in many lands. It should make us think of the great company of Christians of all ages who have observed this rite before us, and from it may well come a great lifting sense of the reality of "the communion of saints."

Finally, there is a sense in which a doctrine of the "real presence" of Christ can be held. Our fellowship is not alone with our fellow Christians. If we have it with them, it is because in a deeper sense both they and we have fellowship with Christ. To go to the Lord's table in the spirit of Christ is to find him there. "Do this in remembrance of me" must be put side by side with, "Lo, I am with you always." It is as one finds the living presence of Christ, whether at the Lord's Supper or in the daily demands of life, that peace and power and newness of life are given.

# Chapter VII

## WHAT IS MAN?

*T*HE POET WHO wrote the eighth psalm, overwhelmed by the greatness of the physical universe and his own littleness in it, cried out to God:

When I consider thy heavens, the work of thy fingers,
The moon and the stars, which thou hast ordained;
What is man, that thou art mindful of him?

Had he known what we know of astronomical space and island universes millions of light-years away, which the great telescopes reveal, he might have been all the more impressed with man's insignificance. He found the answer to his question and put it in the next words:

For thou hast made him but little lower than God,
And crownest him with glory and honor.
Thou makest him to have dominion over the work of
thy hands;
Thou hast put all things under his feet.

Our problem is, Can we still say this of man? Not only has astronomy greatly enlarged our view of the physical world in which man seems but a tiny midget, but the mutual slaughter of millions of men has greatly deflated our confidence in man's ability to master himself or the world. Yet it is basic to Christian faith to see in man dignity, greatness, and kinship to God.

The reason why it is not easy to say clearly just what man is, is the fact that when one begins to describe one aspect of man's nature, another apparently contradictory but equally real aspect presents itself. Then unless both sides are included, the description becomes not only fragmentary but false. The Christian understanding of man can best be stated in four of these paradoxes:

1. Man is both nature and spirit.
2. Man is both free and bound.
3. Man is both child of God and sinner.
4. Man is both transient and eternal.

We shall attempt in this chapter to suggest the meaning of the first three, leaving the fourth until we come to a special chapter on immortality.

## 1. *Man as nature and spirit*

To say that man is nature is simply to say what few people have ever denied—that we each have a body. This body is composed of physical and chemical elements, very intricately related. It has much in common with the bodies of the higher animals, and has a long biological past. Each human body is marvelously equipped with organs of sensation, muscular movement, digestion, circulation, respiration, reproduction, self-repair of injury, and other functions that we seldom think about unless they get out of order. The human body takes longer to mature than the bodies of most of the lower animals, and it will endure an amazing amount of strain, but it wears out in seventy or eighty years.

If we ask whether our bodies are the product of

nature or of God, it is a false alternative, for everything in nature is the handiwork of God. That God has been fashioning the human organism through billions of years of creative labor should not make us think less, but more, highly of it. And the more one learns through biology or physiology of the way it is put together to serve our need, the more we can say with the psalmist:

I will give thanks unto thee; for I am fearfully and
    wonderfully made:
Wonderful are thy works;
And that my soul knoweth right well.

But is the body all? Christian faith affirms vigorously that it is not. In the majestic epic of creation with which Genesis begins, there are three key sentences: "In the beginning God created . . . And God saw that it was good . . . And God created man in his own image, in the image of God created he him." This conviction that man is a living soul made in the divine image is central to our understanding of ourselves and our fellow man. Let us add to this witness from the Old Testament. Jesus' unvarying estimate of the worth of every human soul as a child of God—however weak, sinful, or outcast by men one might be—and we have the foundations of the Christian view of man and his destiny.

The term "soul" has gone out of fashion in many quarters, particularly among psychologists. This is not wholly loss, for it is inaccurate to speak of the soul as a third thing about us that is not mind or body—a mysterious something that cannot be discovered or defined. Nevertheless, when the soul is understood as spirit, or as mind or consciousness in the broadest sense, it means something very real. Perhaps the best way to get at what it means is to think of the difference between the human spirit and all lower forms of animal life. A man can weigh moral issues and make moral decisions, can strive after truth and beauty, can learn from the past experience of the human race and project his aspirations into the long future, can form fellowships with other men for mutual enrichment, can worship God and come into fellowship with him. These capacities make of man a "living soul" in a sense not shared by any other creature, and justify us in assuming with the author of Genesis that man is God's supreme creation made in the divine image.

## 2. Man as free and bound

If we undertake to select one atribute which above all distinguishes human personality from animal life and from the world of physical nature, it is man's freedom. If we glance again at the characteristics named above which make him a soul, we see it is only because man has some freedom of choice that he can decide between good and evil, employ his intelligence to discover truth, become sensitive to beauty, appropriate meanings from the past or project them as goals into the future, increase the values in a society, or come into conscious fellowship with God. God might have chosen to make us automatic puppets or mechanically determined robots, but he chose to make us men with freedom to achieve or mar our destinies.

Freedom is God's supreme gift, though with it comes

inevitably the possibility of its misuse. Without freedom there would be no sin, for "sin lies at the juncture of nature and spirit." Without freedom we should have no responsibility for ignorance or error. But without freedom we should be human machines instead of sons of God. It is freedom that makes us moral beings bearing the divine image.

Nevertheless, we are never wholly free, and it is as serious a mistake to overlook our limitations as to deny the fact of our freedom. Our heredity, our social environment, and our own previous experience have set for us certain paths that are easier to follow than others, though in normal persons the grooves are seldom so fixed that we cannot possibly get out of them. Our bodies, useful servants that they are, are subject to fatigue and disease; they have to be fed and clothed; they will not do all that in our more ambitious moments we ask of them. We live in a physical world which in its basic order cannot be changed, and which in the arrangement of its parts is subject—but never wholly so—to control by human wills. We live in a society of which many aspects—but not every aspect at once—can be altered. On any project we work at, whether it is getting a meal, reading a book, driving a car, controlling the use of atomic energy, or making world peace, human freedom can be exercised effectively only when our limitations, as well as the possibilities open to us, are taken into account.

Some of these limiting factors are established by God in the creation of the world. Such things as gravitation in the physical world, the eventual death of a living organism, the inevitable collapse of a society built on hate and greed, are elements in the way things are made. We had better accept them, for protest will not change them. Others, such as preventable disease, ignorance, poverty, strife, and all manner of social evils, are man-made limitations and by a right use of human freedom can be removed. A large part of what is meant by the coming of God's Kingdom on earth is the lifting of such limitations so that all men, as God's sons, may be free.

### 3. Man as child of God

This brings us to the third great paradox. Man is the child of God, as Jesus taught us to regard him. Otherwise the words "Our Father" would be meaningless. Man is of infinite worth as God's child. But man also is a sinner. Which note shall we put uppermost?

It is essential that we keep a right balance in our judgment of man's nature. Religious humanism and the more extreme forms of liberalism have sometimes made so much of man's power and self-sufficiency that God almost vanished from the picture. Or, if God did not disappear, the difference between God and man became so slight that humility about our status tended to disappear. In contrast with this assumption of the divineness of human nature, the new orthodoxy puts its emphasis on the difference between God and man, and on the sinfulness which always and everywhere corrupts human nature. There is truth in both these positions, and error in both if carried to extremes. We must never forget that it is God who has made us, and not we ourselves; that our lives are in his keeping; that the only appropriate attitude for the Christian is humble worship of God and dependence on our Creator.

Sinners we are, and sinners we remain save for the unmerited, forgiving mercy of God. Nevertheless, we are children of God, and *all* men are his children—made in his image with the stamp of divinity upon their souls.

To hold this belief about man is vital to our Christian outlook and action. Upon it hinge many issues. Take, for example, democracy. Whatever the political system, there can be no real democracy except that which is founded on the conviction that all human beings, of whatever race, or color, or class, or sex, are of supreme worth in God's sight and ought therefore to be treated as persons. This conviction is the only real leverage by which to combat race prejudice, economic exploitation, mass unemployment, forced labor, or other forms of slavery. Only on the basis of the equality and inherent worth of men and women, adults and children, old persons and young, can family fellowship exist. Not until this principle is extended to include the persons of all nations in the family of God, great nations and small, white and colored, victor and vanquished, shall we have an international order founded on the ideal of justice for all—and without this foundation we shall not have peace.

Within our churches our programs of missions, religious education, evangelism, and most of the other activities would be meaningless except for the conviction that all persons are precious to God and are at the same time in need of salvation and capable of being brought to new life in Christ. When Paul wrote,

"There is neither Jew nor Greek, there is neither bond nor free, there is neither male nor female: for ye are all one in Christ Jesus," he uttered truth of far-reaching consequences.

If this is true of our basic human relations, what man thinks of himself is equally important to personal living. The undermining of a sense of meaning and destiny for one's life is one of the most serious aspects of our contemporary scene. From it has come much cynicism, despair, and loss of nerve. Whatever happens, one ought to live with courage, dignity, and hope. One can so live if he thinks of himself as a child of God and, in spite of tragic sin and folly, knows himself to be the object of God's continuing love and care. Lacking this conviction, one is apt to find his stamina slipping and inner resources crumbling before the avalanche of misery that has engulfed our time. Only the union of humility with an awareness of human dignity that is not of our own making but the gift of God, can enable us to transform confusion and chaos into "a time for greatness."

## 4. Man as sinner

But not only is it necessary to preserve a sense of man's dignity as God's child; it is equally, and perhaps even more, necessary to see all men including ourselves as sinners. What, then, do we mean by sin? [1]

There is no single definition of sin, and no list of sins that could be drawn up would be complete. What

[1] Several paragraphs in this section are reprinted from the chapter entitled "The Burden of Our Sin" in *The Dark Night of the Soul.*

is ordinarily thought of as sin, such as lying, stealing, drinking, gambling, may be sinful; but to name such practices does not get anywhere near to the heart of the trouble. That opinions of Christians differ as to the sinfulness of such recreations as card playing and dancing shows the need of something that goes much deeper than the practice itself if we are to judge what is sinful.

In the first place, any act or attitude that is sinful runs counter to the nature of God and the righteous will of God. This is the truth that lies in the often distorted doctrine of human depravity. When we measure even our best acts and aspirations by the standard of God's holy will as revealed in Christ, we all have sinned and come short of the glory of God. The eclipse of the concept of sin during the brief ascendancy of humanistic liberalism was a direct outgrowth of our failure to take seriously God's holiness and the rigor of his moral demands. When man becomes the measure of all things, we talk of "cultural lags" and "antisocial behavior." When God is restored to his rightful place of primacy in human thought, sin, our ancient enemy, again is seen to be our ever-present and most malignant foe.

In the second place, any sin, whether of overt act or inner attitude, presupposes freedom to do or to be otherwise. To the extent that a person really does what he must do or is what he must be, *and cannot help himself*, to that extent he is victim and not sinner. As nobody is wholly free, so nobody is wholly depraved. But the other side of this comforting truth is that one rarely, if ever, is wholly helpless and therefore free

100

from guilt. In almost every situation there is freedom enough left to do better than one does. Certainly if we view life, not as separate incidents, but as a whole, nobody ever reaches the upper limits of his freedom. In those large areas of choice which God has given us but within which we do not choose according to his will, we sin and stand under his righteous judgment.

In the third place, sin presupposes a knowledge of good and evil adequate to form a basis of choice. According to the ancient but wonderfully meaningful story of the Fall, there was no sin in Eden until our first parents, discontented with their human lot and desiring to be "as God," ate from the tree of knowledge of good and evil. Such knowledge is at once our bond of kinship with divinity and our undoing. The demand of our faith is not ignorance, but humble dedication of such knowledge as we have to God and action by it in accordance with his will.

And in the fourth place, sin, according to the Christian frame of thought, involves at the same time relation to our neighbor and to God. As the Christian requirement of love links love of God and love of neighbor in a twofold Great Commandment from which neither element can be dropped, so sin against neighbor through lack of human love is sin against God. The distinctive character of Jesus' ethics lies in the fact that for him religion and morals were all of one piece. To do the will of his Father and to serve those in need were for him not two requirements but one, a supremely costly but supremely joyous adventure in self-giving love.

When these four requirements are put together, at least the outlines of the meaning of sin become clear. There is a sinful state of pride and rebellion against God from which not even the most saintly soul is wholly clear. There are sinful attitudes and acts, such as anger, avarice, lust, killing, stealing, adultery, in which a person free enough so that he could feel and do otherwise chooses to obey evil impulses instead of good. There are sins of omission that arise, not so much from positive sinful impulses as from something that may be even more serious because more subtle—from indifference; from moral dullness, laziness, and flabbiness; from lethargy and complacency where we ought to be sensitive to the needs and feelings of others; from ignorance at points where we could know what we ought to do if we took pains to try to know.

There are also what are usually called social sins, such as race prejudice, economic injustice, tyranny, persecution, and war. In such situations one may not *feel* like much of a sinner, for the sin is so commonly practiced and its effects so spread out that one's sense of guilt is dulled. Nevertheless, the consequences of such sins are often far more serious than of private and more easily recognized sins, for the effects are multiplied manyfold in complex social relations. Actually no clear distinction can be drawn between individual and social sins, for every sin proceeds from the attitude of an individual, and every sin in its consequences affects somebody else besides the sinner.

All sin roots in self-love, in preferring to have our own way when we ought to love God and our neighbor. Everybody knows what this means—or ought to, for we all do it! The moral life even for the best of men is a continual struggle against selfishness. This simple but serious fact throws light on some otherwise difficult theological ideas.

There is born in all of us, not "original sin" as a hereditary corruption passed on from Adam's guilt, but a biological tendency to self-centeredness. This is as natural and unsinful in little children as is the impulse to eat or sleep or cry from discomfort. It is a useful endowment, not only for self-preservation, but for the growth of personality through the relating of all experience to the self. But such self-centeredness, though very necessary, is very dangerous, and in adult life easily passes over into willful selfishness. If uncurbed, it becomes the self-love which is the root of all other sins and of most of our unhappiness.

The forms such self-love takes, in the ordinary events of living, are manifold. It shows itself in desire to have our own way regardless of the wishes or rights or needs of others; in the narrowing of interests to what immediately touches us; in thirst for personal recognition, compliments, and applause; in eagerness in conversation or action always to occupy the center of the stage; in jealousy of others who secure recognition or privileges or goods we want; in self-pity; in peevishness and petty complaint when things do not go as we would have them. These are, at best, unlovely traits when we see them in others. As indications that we love ourselves more than we love our neighbor or our Lord, they are evidences of sin so life strangling that God alone can give release.

So firmly do the chains of self-centeredness enmesh us that we cannot by will power break their hold. Whether selfishness takes the form of callous indifference or of positive self-seeking, being ashamed of it will not release us. Shame may be a step toward repentance, but it cannot of itself deliver us and may serve only to increase our despair. This is the way Paul felt about it when he exclaimed:

The good which I would I do not: but the evil which I would not, that I practise. . . . I find then the law, that, to me who would do good, evil is present. For I delight in the law of God after the inward man: but I see a different law in my members, warring against the law of my mind, and bringing me into captivity under the law of sin which is in my members. Wretched man that I am! who shall deliver me out of the body of this death? [2]

God alone can save us. But can God? Only if we yield our wills to him and in repentance and faith lay hold upon his forgiveness. If we do not, our self-love is "unpardonable," not because God does not desire to pardon us, but because we do not make the commitment of faith which alone opens the way to his forgiving mercy. God cannot meet us if we block the path. The "sin of unbelief" is no theoretical rejection of God's existence; it is the deadlier atheism of preferring our way to his, of choosing to live by our own desires and standards to the rejection of his righteous will. If persisted in, it means the death of

[2] Romans 7:19-24.

our higher life and of all that is potentially best within us.

God gives release. When Paul asked the question, "Who shall deliver me from the body of this death?" he answered it in his next words, "I thank God through Jesus Christ our Lord." By the beginning of the next chapter he was saying: "There is therefore now no condemnation to them that are in Christ Jesus. For the law of the Spirit of life in Christ Jesus made me free from the law of sin and death." [3] And at the end of the chapter he pours out his spirit in one of the most glorious paeons of victory in all literature: "Who shall separate us from the love of Christ? shall tribulation, or anguish, or persecution, or famine, or nakedness, or peril, or sword? . . . Nay, in all these things we are more than conquerors through him that loved us." [4]

This is the story of Christian conquest through the ages. Let us see in our next chapter how we may hope to find it.

[3] Romans 8:1-2.
[4] Romans 8:35-37.

Chapter VIII

SALVATION

*T*HE WORD "salvation" has largely gone out of fashion in our time. This does not mean that the desire to be saved has vanished; for, apart from any religious meaning, the hope of salvation is as wide as the sweep of human desire. Every advertisement appeals to it. This new kitchen equipment will save you from drudgery, this brand of fruit juice from vitamin deficiency, this deodorant from social embarrassment and a lonely spinsterhood! Ranging all the way from "success" books to tell how to be saved from unpopularity to books on the present world situation, our literature is full of attempts to point the way to salvation. Why, then, are we so squeamish about it in religion?

Even among many people otherwise favorable to religion, the idea of salvation is in poor standing. This is chiefly for two reasons. First, the term is not well understood. From revival sermons of an earlier day it has come to mean a sharp separation of the saved from the damned, with the saved going to the bliss of heaven while sinners forever burn in hell. This seems so inconsistent with the God of love revealed in Christ that this idea of salvation has been widely given up, but with nothing to put in its place. In the second place, those who see a more appropriate meaning in terms of the peace, joy, and spiritual victory of the Christian are often still at a loss to know how to lay hold upon it for themselves.

We shall, therefore, attempt in this chapter first to say what Christian salvation is, and then to suggest how it may be found.

## 1. *The meaning of salvation*

In its most elementary meaning, "to be saved" means to be rescued, delivered, made safe from something we ought to be rid of. As we saw in the last chapter, the most persistent evil we need to be freed from is sin; hence, salvation from sin has always been at the center of Christian faith and life. But we need also to be delivered from frustration, inadequacy, destructive inner conflict, despair. There is no full salvation or spiritual victory unless there is a lifting of the chains, not only of sin, but of futility. The saved person feels himself "more than conqueror," through a power not his own, over the forces within and without that assail and crush the spirit.

This suggests that salvation is not merely a negative process. It is more than getting rid of something—whether sin or frustration; it is positive, joyous spiritual health. As the German word for it, *Heil*, suggests, it means health, healing, wholeness of living. We are saved *from* whatever separates us from God and our best living; we are saved *to* the kind of life in which we can work with God victoriously and zestfully to do his will.

This does not mean that we are saved to complete sinlessness or entire efficiency in our attempts to serve

107

God. As long as we live, we are human, and both our good intentions and our accomplishments have human limits. But there is a vast difference between a life that is halting, stumbling, warped by its own selfishness, and a life that is free and strong in the power of God. It is to this fullness of life, with a new center of loyalty, a new strength, and a new sense of direction, that we are saved.

What, then, are we saved *by?* This can be said in a sentence but requires a lifetime for its understanding. We are saved by the grace of God—by the free, gracious, outpouring of God's love upon us and his forgiveness when we repent of our sin and turn to him for cleansing and strength. We do not save ourselves; it is God that saves us. But this does not mean that it costs nothing on our part. God can save us only as we meet his conditions and open our lives to receive his power.

Salvation, according to Christian faith, is for both this life and the next. Both are important. However, we shall leave the discussion of salvation in the next life to a later chapter, when we take up the belief in immortality, for it belongs in that field. Also, since salvation for the next world has often bulked so large as to obscure its meaning for this one, it may be useful to shift the emphasis. If salvation now is real, its continuance to the next life is probable; if salvation made no difference here, no amount of speculation about heaven or hell could possibly ring true.

## 2. *Terms, old and new*

The meaning of salvation may become clearer if we look at some of the terms connected with it. Many of the older ones have been given up because they were so encrusted with tradition. Rather than discard them, we had better rub off the dust and see what permanent truth lies hidden in them.

First, what is a "lost soul?" To be lost means simply to be out of right relations, as a lost book is one not in its proper place on the library shelf, a lost coin is one that has fallen out of the purse where it belongs, a lost child is one that has strayed from its home and does not know the way back. In a religious sense, to be "lost" is to be out of right relations with God—separated from fellowship with him through our own indifference and self-will, cut off from our own best living because we have cut ourselves off from its sources in God. Jesus told some immortal parables that illustrate this—about a lost sheep, a lost piece of silver, a lost boy that we call the prodigal son.[1] Only as these were eagerly and lovingly sought after and restored to where they belonged were they saved. This is the basic Christian meaning of God's love that yearns always to save the lost.

But the term "lost soul" has another meaning that fits most of us. To be "lost" when confronted by any situation is to be confused, bewildered, unable to decide what to do next or which way to turn. From this kind of lostness also we need salvation. George Matheson in his hymn "Make Me a Captive, Lord," describes it perfectly:

[1] Luke 15.

> My heart is weak and poor
>   Until it master find;
> It has no spring of action sure—
>   It varies with the wind.

Only as we let God direct and master us can we find freedom to go forward with assurance. As was suggested earlier, salvation from the lostness of inadequacy and futility must accompany salvation from sin if life is to be made whole.

Next, what do we mean by "conversion?" To be converted," as its derivation suggests, means to "turn around," to turn about from a self-centered to a God-centered life. This turning may be a very gradual process, involving many decisions and growth by almost imperceptible stages. Or the turning may be sudden, dramatic, and overwhelming in emotional power. Though the term "evangelism" has sometimes been used for conversion of the second type only, it ought not to be thus limited. A person is as truly converted if the process takes place with relatively little emotional fireworks and over a considerable period as he is if it happens all at once. In both types there is preparation, for sudden conversion is the rapid crystallization of factors previously imbedded in the subconscious mind—as Paul on the Damascus road had been "kicking against the pricks" ever since he witnessed the stoning of Stephen. In both types there is decision, for there is no real conversion until one decides for himself to try to obey God and to open his life to the power of God. When this happens and one resolves earnestly by the help of God to live henceforth, not for oneself alone, but for God and for other people, a change takes place that is the greatest thing that can happen to any soul.[2]

"Regeneration" is another word that is no longer heard very often. It means to be "born again," to come to new life through the power of God in Christ. This may seem to us too mysterious to grasp, as it did to Nicodemus, who came to Jesus by night. When Jesus said to him, "Except one be born anew, he cannot see the kingdom of God," Nicodemus—literalist like ourselves—cried out, "How can a man be born when he is old?"[3] Yet through the centuries millions of Christians have demonstrated by their lives that it is possible in maturity to "come alive," and in the midst of a humdrum existence to find a fresh vitality born of the Spirit of God, which makes life meaningful and good.

"Redemption" is another great word for Christian salvation, the meaning of which was explained in chapter five. As we saw, this was taken in the Bible originally from the metaphor of redeeming, or buying back, a slave in the market place. However, it means to us now the whole great process of the salvation of the world through the yearning, merciful love of God— a process in which he calls us to work with him in love, as followers of Christ, to bring individuals and

---

[2] The question is often raised as to whether religious education should eliminate the need for conversion. It can make the sudden type unnecessary, but, even with the best of Christian nurture, personal decision is still necessary.

[3] John 3.

nations to his way. Redemption is God's supreme gift. As the prayer of general thanksgiving in *The Book of Common Prayer* puts it: "We bless thee for our creation, preservation, and all the blessings of this life; but above all, for thine inestimable love in the redemption of the world by our Lord Jesus Christ."

"Justification" has its setting in a court of law. We are "justified by faith," as Paul put it, to "have peace with God through our Lord Jesus Christ"[4] when in repentance and humble trust we accept the mercy and forgiveness of God and know that he holds nothing against us in spite of our sin. Justification is meaningless apart from God's condemnation of sin; but if God's judgment is as real as both the Bible and the events of history show, justification is the other side of it. Knowing ourselves to be sinners, we find our peace in spite of guilt, not by evasion or by frantically doing good works, but by repentance. Seeing our sin as evil as it is and knowing that the God whose infinite mercy we see in Christ does not charge it up against us, we can go forward. A better analogy than the law court by which to understand this is the human parent who suffers in love because a child has done wrong, yet in love forgives and goes on trusting.

Forgiveness does, and does not, cancel sin. Every sin leaves its scars of evil consequences, and forgiveness does not change these effects. They are there to spur us on to make whatever amends we can. But, no longer weighed down with a sense of guilt, with a new

[4] Romans 5:1.

vitality born of gratitude the forgiven sinner can make a fresh start toward the doing of God's will.

"Sanctification" does not mean, as is often supposed, that one ever gets to the point where he no longer sins. To assert such a view is very dangerous, for it leads to self-righteousness and a false sense of moral security. Even the best Christians must fight moral battles which they sometimes lose and must repeatedly ask for forgiveness. The term may well be avoided for this reason. But if one wants to use it, it should mean the dedication of oneself to God and the hallowing of all life through the power of the Holy Spirit. To the mature Christian, as he seeks to live and work in fellowship with God, there is a sanctity and holiness about everything he does which seems not to come from his own effort but to be the gift of God. If he has a conscience sensitive to God's demands to keep him humble, such a sense of the abiding presence of God is a source of great joy and strength.

We have been looking at some old terms; it may be best to take a glance at some more modern ones. "Integration of personality" means wholeness of personality—the bringing together of life's disjointed fragments into a unity. In this unity the conflicts that were tearing one's life apart and keeping it weak and ineffective are replaced by inner security and strength. This is probably what Jesus did in his miracles of healing, particularly those in which he cast out demons, and he describes it perfectly in the words he spoke repeatedly, "Thy faith hath made thee whole." It is a tragedy of our time that psychologists and educators who have so much to say about the integration of personality have often so small a place for life's greatest integrating force—Christian faith.

"Commitment" and "dedication" are fairly common terms to indicate the giving of oneself to a new center of loyalty. They ought not to be regarded as in contrast with conversion, but as a part of it. It is immaterial whether one speaks of dedication to God or to Christ, provided he means by it the commitment of life to the God revealed and brought to us in Christ.

"Religious awakening" implies that one has been asleep and is now awake to the beauty and power of the Christian gospel. "Orientation," like "conversion," means that a life askew and and off center needs to be turned around and set right.

All of these terms, requiring less definition than the older ones, have their place. It is better to use them than to confuse or close people's minds by words against which emotional barriers have been set up. Yet it is to be doubted whether any one of these terms has the depth of meaning to be found in those that have come from the Bible and have been used through the centuries. There is danger, also, that in using the more modern terms the emphasis may be put too much on what we do and not enough on what God does. Yet in our time, as in Paul's, we must be "all things to all men" if we would by all means save some.

### 3. What must we do to be saved?

There is no more searching question that anyone can ask than the one which the Philippian jailer put to Paul, "What must I do to be saved?" Paul's answer,

"Believe on the Lord Jesus Christ," is bedrock for Christian faith and experience, and in chapter five we tried to discover something as to what this means. But even when one knows that he ought to be a follower of Christ and sees that through Christ others find a power that transforms their living, the question still remains as to how to enter into this experience.

The purpose of this section is to try to trace the steps one must take who would appropriate for himself the power and grace of God channeled to us through Christ. There is no exact technique for entering into this new fellowship with God any more than there is for falling in love with another human person. Yet there are some things required of us—some things to do and some not to do. Understanding the process will not cause it to happen in us, but misunderstanding may block the way.

The first step is awareness of need. In the story of the prodigal son it was when the boy saw that he lacked something and said, "I will arise and go to my Father," that his redemption began. As long as a person thinks that he is good enough or has enough, not even God himself can break down this wall of indifference. We must open the door before God can help us. "Behold, I stand at the door and knock." This requirement has been vividly portrayed in Holman Hunt's great picture of Christ knocking at a door which can be opened only from the inside.

The awareness of need which is essential to the finding of God comes most often, if not always, through a human agency. This is true in two senses. God to save us came to earth in the human form of Jesus, and the

115

more we live with the personality of Jesus as we find the record in the Bible, the more we see our own littleness and are challenged to want to be something better. This is why there is no substitute for acquaintance with Jesus through the New Testament. But in a second sense God uses human agencies, as we see what Christ means in the lives and words of his followers, past and present. The stimulus that awakens us to our own need may be a book, a sermon, a service of worship and prayer, a conversation or discussion, the lift that comes from a group of Christians united in a common task, the story of Christian courage and sacrifice under testing, or, most potent of all, the influence of the daily living and personal friendship of a great Christian. In short, the thing that wakes us up can be anything that shows the difference Christ makes in the lives of persons who place him at the center of their faith and loyalty.

This awareness of need can come at any time, during the smoothest existence or the most stormy. We are especially open to this discovery when something occurs to upset our familiar pattern of life—a great new responsibility, such as marriage, parenthood, or a new vocation; an emergency, such as failure, illness, separation by physical absence or death from someone that is loved. Even our hardest experiences and darkest hours, as many found during the strains of war, can be avenues to the discovery of our own need and the availability of God's limitless power.

The second step, growing out of the first without clear separation, is *surrender of will*. The term "surrender" sounds strange to modern ears, for it reflects a mood at variance with the prevailing mental climate. We want to be masters of our fate and captains of our souls—that is, if we still believe there is a soul of which to be captain. The idea of surrendering to anybody or anything suggests servility, and we do not want to be servile.

Until we can shake ourselves out of this mood, no very widespread revival of religion is likely to take place. What makes religion *religion* is willingness to worship, to bow in humility before an utterly holy deity, and to subordinate self to the service of that deity. As long as religion is used as a means to an end— even though a very worthy end—it eludes us. "Using" religion means trying to make God do what men want done, which is not religion at all, but magic. "Being religious" means subjecting man's will to the will of God.

How to know what God wills is less simple than is sometimes supposed. We cannot safely trust tradition or intuition by itself. The will of God is a matter to be discerned in the light of our most sensitive insights and most reasoned judgments. Prayer is needed; so is weighing of the probable consequences of any proposed act. Neither is a substitute for the other, and the attempt to make one do duty for the other is neither good sense nor good religion.[5]

To decide what to do is important; to be willing to do it is indispensable. Without such surrender of will there can be no conversion, no turning from a self-centered to a God-centered life. With it self-will does

[5] See chapter XI, section 3 for further discussion of this problem.

not wholly disappear, but the self is enlarged and enriched by the inclusion of many interests hitherto rejected. Persons and causes to be served move from the outer circle to the center of attention; and with these and God in the center, life gains a new stability and strength.

This richness and stability are acquired only at the cost of repentance. God "delivers us from evil," but deliverance and forgiveness come only when we have done all that we can to open the way. Repentance means facing our sins squarely, without morbidness and without self-delusion. It means confession of our sins to God, and often also to trusted human persons, but it does not mean a public advertising of them. It means earnest self-searching, sincere contrition, and so far as possible making amends for the harm one has done to others. Whoever is unwilling to pay this price can get no farther.

The third step has already been suggested. This is *deliverance*. No magical perfection ensues, but an increase in poise and power. There is a paradoxical freedom here, for by the surrender of self-will one gains a higher freedom. This third step, like all the others, is one in which openness of spirit must be joined with active effort. God delivers, but delivers only those who will accept what is offered. God saves the person who is "lost," but only him who is willing to find the way.

Such deliverance means far more than a comfortable emotional glow. When it is only this, it soon cools and disappears. It means reorganization of life from the inside out, and from the bottom up. Failure to rec-

118

ognize this fact has led to the gruesome practice of counting the number of souls saved in meetings, and it has helped to fill church rosters with people whom the rest of the world call hypocrites.

Acceptance of deliverance means earnest, persistent grappling with the habitual sins that hold us in their grip—not always flagrant offenses against the moral code, but the more insidious and therefore more dangerous sins of a bad temper, faultfinding, jealousy, arrogance, irresponsibility, laziness, self-delusion, petty-mindedness. To overcome these is both to take up one's cross daily and to rejoice thankfully in victory.

The fourth step, therefore, is *spiritual growth*. This does not mean either a sudden or a final sinlessness. It does mean in the dedicated Christian the progressive achievement of moral victory and the abundant life. It means increasing spiritual insight and increasing moral earnestness, fed by the life of worship and empowered by, as well as for, the doing of constructive tasks of human service. Without such expression in life there is no religious vitality.

The person who achieves most fully the experience which has been described will be the last to boast of being a Christian. But others will call him this and will see in him a living witness to the power of Christ, who is "the author and perfecter of our faith."

Putting from us spiritual arrogance and indifference, we must sense our need, surrender our wills in repentance, accept God's deliverance, and live the life of victory over sin and chaos. There need be nothing dramatic or spectacular about this. But it does not happen by accident. These steps suggest the route which the great religious spirits have always followed. These are the steps which need to be taken today if we are to find power in God to grapple with the problems of our time.

## Chapter IX

## PRAYER AND PROVIDENCE

Does god answer prayer? What is prayer? What things have we a right to ask God for? Can we pray for material as well as spiritual blessings? What about prayer for other people? What does it mean to pray "in Christ's name"? Does God have a plan for our lives? Does prayer make any difference in what happens? Such questions come crowding one upon another, and suggest problems that need to be cleared up before one can pray with full assurance. Let us see what can be said about them.

### 1. *God's relation to his children*

It is the Christian faith that God is a personal, all-wise, and all-loving Father; that he loves and cares for us as individuals; that he knows our needs and seeks at all times to help us; that he has a good purpose and a destiny for our lives. All of these convictions together give one a doctrine of providence—not a belief that God manipulates the universe upon request, but a deep assurance that everything that matters is safe in God's keeping.

Each of these affirmations sheds light on the meaning of prayer and the possibility of its answer. If God is our Father, though he works through orderly natural processes, he never works mechanically or in detachment from human need. If he is concerned with individuals, he is not interested simply in the human race but in each one of us. To suppose that God could not care for each of us because there are so many people in the world is to place upon him human limitations; but, let us remember, he is God, not man! If he knows our need and seeks to help us, we do not have to give him information, but we do need through prayer to place ourselves in an attitude to be helped. If God has a will and purpose for our lives, the most important thing anybody can do is to try to discover and obey God's will. The essence of all true prayer is, "Not my will, but thine, be done."

If this is our conviction, we are ready to inquire further as to what prayer is.

## 2. *What is prayer?*

I know of no better definition than that of the *Westminster Shorter Catechism*, "Prayer is the offering up of our desires unto God for things agreeable to His will." This puts the focus where it belongs—on God and his will. But it also suggests that the human side has its place; it is "our desires"—the deep and dominant desires of the soul—that we offer up to him.

Some substitutes for prayer must be ruled out on this basis. The reading or repetition of words, whether those of the Lord's Prayer or the *Upper Room* or some treasury of prayers of the ages, is not by itself an act of prayer. This is not to condemn the use of aids, for they may be very helpful channels of prayer. But it is the response of the soul, the offering up of our desires unto

God, that makes such words *prayer* rather than muscular exercise. It is at this simple but all-important point that much of our alleged praying collapses.

Reacting from the pitfall of such mechanical repetition, others would make of prayer so much a matter of mood that words seem unnecessary. To be "in tune with the Infinite," to "feel the surge of the oversoul," and similar expressions are an attempt to get away from particularizing prayer in a chatty fashion, as one might talk to another human being. This reaction is based on a good impulse but can easily be carried too far. To try to make of prayer *merely* a matter of mood is to banish the mood and give way to vagueness. Prayer is not prayer unless it centers in communication and response.

It is at this point that "prayer" is to be differentiated from "worship." For most practical purposes these two terms can be used interchangeably. However, if one wishes to use them with strict accuracy, worship is an attitude of reverence toward deity, which may be conceived impersonally, and no response is presupposed. There is worship in every religion; there is prayer only where it is believed that God—or the gods—can answer. It lies at the heart of Christian faith that God is personal, a Supreme Person with whom we may communicate through the spiritual faculties he has given us. There is great truth in Tennyson's words:

"Speak to Him, thou, for He hears, and Spirit with
    Spirit can meet—
Closer is He than breathing, and nearer than hands and
    feet."

There are various activities so closely allied to prayer and worship that they tend to become substitutes. There is the sense of beauty, particularly the lifting power of the beauty of nature and of great music. Through these channels men have often found God; but not usually, if ever, until they have found him elsewhere and have learned to make beauty an aid to worship rather than a substitute for it. There is meditation—honest self-examination or reflection on some vital theme. This can be a very fruitful part of prayer, but it is not prayer unless it is centered in God and his will. There is labor for God and good causes, which ought to be the fruit of prayer but too often replaces it. Even Christian leaders sometimes fall into such a feverish state of serving God that they forget to seek his strength, by which to serve him well.

### 3. *For what shall we pray?*

There is a natural movement in both public and private prayer which suggests the range of things that make it up.

Prayer begins in worship—in *adoration, praise,* and *thanksgiving* to God. This is necessary to cast the mood outward from self, and upward toward God. But the contemplation of God and his goodness brings—or should bring—a sense of our own unworthiness. Thus the second step is *confession*—a vital part of prayer too often slurred over. Here belong rigorous, even painful self-examination and the stripping off of all excuses and alibis as we try to see ourselves in the light of God's high demands. Confession should lead on to *petition—*

124

petition for forgiveness but also for wisdom, strength, and all the good gifts needful for our fullest living. When we ask for ourselves we should ask also for others, and we move to *intercession*. But to ask is blasphemy unless we intend to act, and should lead on to *dedication or* commitment. This is the point for crystallization of the resolution to go forward in more Christlike living, in greater service to those for whom we pray, in greater obedience to God's will. With a final word of the *assurance* of God's victory ("Thine is the kingdom") and the *ascription* of the prayer to Christ ("in Christ's name" or "through Jesus Christ our Lord"), our period of prayer is rounded out.

I do not mean to imply that no prayer is "right" unless it contains all of these moods and in just this order! God demands of us no fixed mold. Yet all of these are essential elements in prayer; and if we habitually neglect any of them, something is bound to be lacking. Let us now run through this scheme again, pausing for a word on some of the questions that emerge.

About the duty and privilege of adoring and praising God there cannot be much question. The psalmist had it right when he said, "I have set the Lord always before me." [1] If we mean to pray at all, in any sense that is truly prayer and not merely self-indulgence, we shall center our prayer in the worship of God. In spite of all the fun that has been poked at a time-honored phrase, it *is* man's chief end to glorify God! This is true both of our

[1] Psalm 16:8.

acting and our praying. Forgetfulness of this fact has been largely responsible for the self-centered worldliness, and hence for the collapse, of modern society.

Have we a right to thank God for bountiful blessings when so many suffer? Not without being sensitively aware of the agony of the world, penitent for our share in causing it, responsive to the call of God to act redemptively. "To whom much is given, of him will much be required."

What shall we confess? We must not stop with the more overt sins, which most "good people"—by which we generally mean respectable people—do not commit. The grosser sins are the subtle sins of indifference, evasion, pettiness, compromise, self-seeking, jealousy, irritation, discouragement. One *may* need even to repent of sin of excessive self-condemnation, which comes from harboring a sense of guilt instead of laying our sin before God in trust of his forgiving mercy.

For what shall we make petition? For a sense of God's presence and the opportunity to serve him—this above all else. But this is not all. If we believe that God controls the universe and cares for persons, we have a right to pray for many things needed for our fullest living—a healthy body, recovery from illness, enough to eat and to live on, an education, a chance for useful and congenial work, a happy family life, a world at peace. If we can judge God's will at all, we can believe that he wants all men to have these things. They ought to be prayed for and worked for prayerfully. Jesus taught us to pray,

"Give us this day our daily bread." By this he could scarcely have meant spiritual bread alone, for the spirit depends on so many material factors that no sharp separation is possible.

If our prayer seems to have no answer, we had better conclude, not that such good gifts are contrary to God's will, but that we have not worked hard enough for them. Prayer without work is sacrilege if there are things we ought to do. Or it may be that there stand in the way physical or social forces which God cannot set aside without running counter to the orderly processes of his world. Even Jesus had to pray in the garden, "My Father, if it be possible. . . ." [2] The best prayer is not that of clamorous desire even for good things, but a prayer for grace to accept, if necessary, the denial of our desires and for strength to live fruitfully with what we can have.

Is prayer for others legitimate? Many are troubled as to whether God can, or will, influence persons at a distance in response to our praying except by stirring us to do something for them. If it were *only* the latter, intercessory prayer would still be justified by its fruits! But if God can help us by imparting power when we pray, it is reasonable to believe also that he imparts this power to others who are willing to receive it. We are inclined in our time to make of such prayer too much of a problem. For Jesus it was not a problem but a God-given opportunity. It was his loving concern for other men that led him to pray for them, even for his

[2] Matthew 26:39.

enemies, as naturally as he prayed for himself. If we believe that God intends us to live together in a great society—one family as God's sons—we can hardly doubt that he desires us to pray for one another.

About the prayer of commitment the chief problem is not an intellectual one. It is whether we mean it enough to act, at whatever the cost, in response to our resolve. The assurance of God's ultimate triumph is part of our faith as Christians, for we should not pray, "Thy kingdom come," unless we could also affirm, "Thine is the kingdom, the power, and the glory." But this faith makes high demands.

The closing ascription "in Christ's name" is by no means the barren phrase we sometimes make of it. Still less is it a magical incantation, as if to ask "what ye will" with this formula attached would guarantee fulfillment. To ask in Christ's name is to ask in the spirit of Christ, to ask what Jesus would pray for in our place, to ask with Jesus' insight into the nature of God and his ways with men. If we pray in Christ's name, we shall not pray for the trivial or the evil, for selfish gain, for vengeance on our enemies, for the upsetting of the universe in our private interest. To pray in Christ's name is to endeavor to be more Christlike both in our praying and our living. This prayer God always answers if we let him.

For what, then, should we pray? There is no simple answer, but a useful principle is, "Anything we truly need; anything appropriate to the nature of God; anything we can ask in the spirit of Christ." To apply these standards is at once to rule out many things that are selfish, nonessential, impossible of fulfillment in the kind of world God has placed us in, unworthy of the God revealed in Jesus. Yet large areas remain. We have beyond question the right and duty to ask God to impart to us his good gifts as we meet the conditions to receive them. Courage, strength, wisdom, inner calm, an abiding sense of God's nearness, are the most precious gifts God can bestow. No better list has ever been drawn up than Paul's "fruit of the Spirit"—love, joy, peace, long-suffering, kindness, goodness, faithfulness, meekness, and self-control.

## 4. *Providence*

At the beginning of this chapter the outlines of a doctrine of providence were suggested, and its central meaning has been implied throughout the book. However, we must examine it more closely, for the problem of answered and unanswered prayer hinges on it.

"Providence," as the derivation of the word suggests, means that God "sees before" and "looks out for" us.[8] One of the greatest Christians I ever knew was a woman who met every disappointment and trouble that came to her with the words, "There's always a way provided." She had never studied theology, but she had a doctrine of providence that helped her to live bravely and usefully in the midst of circumstances that would have crushed many people.

[8] From the Latin *pro*, "before" or "in behalf of," and *videre*, "to see" or "to look."

In our idea of providence we have to steer between two pitfalls. On the one hand, we must not surrender belief in the loving care of God for every individual. To do so would be to give up our faith in the personal Father-God whom Jesus worshiped and served. His striking references to the birds of the air and the lilies of the field, to the sparrow that does not fall to the ground without the Father's notice, drive home his conviction that God cares for every person and that no one who puts his trust in God need be afraid. It was his trust in God's ever-loving providence that prompted him to say, "Ask, and it shall be given you; seek, and ye shall find; knock, and it shall be opened unto you." But on the other hand, we must not suppose that God changes his mind upon entreaty, or shows partiality in meting out his favors. As Jesus tells us in the Sermon on the Mount, God's love is broad enough so that he makes his sun shine on the evil and the good, and sends rain on the just and the unjust. God would be untrue to himself, and something less than God, if he made provision *only* for those who prayed.

Thus it is essential to combine in our idea of providence both the personal interest of God for every individual and the inclusiveness of his love. The first of these puts vitality into prayer by assuring us that God hears and cares. But the second is equally necessary to keep us from supposing self-righteously that *we* more than others are beloved of God and the special recipients of his bounty. It is a dangerous distortion of the idea of providence to suppose that every calamity that befalls someone else, such as illness, accident, or death, is due to God's indifference or anger, while every good fortune we have is an evidence of his special favor.

To get at the foundation of this, we have to distinguish between two meanings of providence. First, there is a *general providence* in which all men share. When God created the world, he "saw that it was good." One of these elements of goodness we see in the very impartiality of the sun and rain, for the world would soon be crazy chaos if only good people—or those who prayed for it—got good weather! The orderliness that makes science possible; the beauty of nature; its nourishing sustenance in food, air, water, and materials for shelter; the electric, and even the atomic, power available for human needs—these are aspects of God's general providence. Others we find in the joys of family life, friendship, work, play, zest for knowledge—gifts not assured to everybody, but here for the taking if one will pursue them. Prayer makes a difference in the way we use such gifts of God, but even without prayer his general providence would be present. "In him we live, and move, and have our being."

This is as far as some would go. But if God really cares for each individual, it is reasonable as well as Christian to believe that there are also *special providences.*

There are two senses in which the care of God is "special." One is the "special-to-me" feeling that accompanies fellowship with God. Not that others may not have similar comradeship, but in my own experience—or yours—there is something unique, individual, to oneself alone. A deep experience of prayer, however much shared with other persons, has an element in it that nobody but God can share. This is true of any close relation between human friends, but it appears on a higher level in our communion with God. To pray for God's presence is not to deny his continuing presence in nature and the ordinary activities of life, but to open one's spirit to this intimate, individual fellowship. With this sense of God's presence, everything that happens seems to have more of divine significance in it than would otherwise be discerned.

But this is not all. If God's relation to the world and to us is personal, there must also be special answers to prayer. If the world is one of order, not of caprice or mechanical indifference, such answers will come through the orderly processes God has established, not in violation of them. We cannot, therefore, expect that every prayer for particular happenings—however sincerely uttered—will be answered as we desire. Some sick persons prayed for will die; some beloved sons caught in the toils of war will be killed. This is what death and war mean. To supppose that by prayer alone such events can surely be averted is to try to force God to do our bidding, and thus to resort to magic instead of prayer. Nevertheless, we do not live in a closed system within which everything is inevitably determined. Our lives are permeated with purpose, and every moment events that otherwise would not happen take place because of human purposes. For example, I write these words and you read them in response to purpose within a world of order. If with our limited human powers we are able to make things happen in a world of order without violating any natural laws, it is folly to suppose that God cannot!

We ought, therefore, not only in emergencies but in the everyday events of life to pray for whatever seems fitting. The belief in special providences, when safeguarded by a proper sense of what fits the nature of God and how he works in the world to help us, has sound foundations. And it appears justified by the results. Hosts of praying Christians testify, not only to guidance and strength in the inner life, but to the actual shaping of events far beyond what can be charged to mere coincidence.

Finally, what about the fact—very evident to any honest mind—of unanswered prayer? There is no single explanation that covers every case. Some petitions, as was suggested earlier, are denied because we have not tried hard enough to answer them ourselves. Some are for things that cannot be granted in God's kind of world —as, for example, a prayer for peace that overlooks all the steps that must be taken to establish the foundations of peace. Some petitions that we call prayer are merely self-centered clamor that our wills, not God's, be done. Sometimes the answer is "no" to teach us to seek something better. Some prayers are humble, earnest, God-centered, and still apparently unanswered.

When we have gone as far as we can with the problem, there are still areas of mystery, for we are not as wise as God. Yet there is a great ground of certainty to stand upon. No prayer that seeks in humility and trust to find God's power and providence for our lives is futile. Paul did not have his "thorn in the flesh" removed; yet God's providence so encompassed him that in illness, imprisonment, shipwreck, and superhuman labors he was able to say, "I have learned, in whatsoever state I am, therein to be content." Even a "thorn in the spirit" may not be wholly removed, for the body is so interwoven with the spirit that there are conditions under which spiritual victory seems to elude us.[4] Yet there is no situation in which prayer and a trust in God's providence do not matter. However dark the night, we can know that God is with us in the dark. We can know that, though we may be defeated, God cannot be. We can know that any evil may be turned to good account in stronger character and richer service. When we know that "there's always a way provided," we can stand instead of slipping—and move a little forward.

[4] See *The Dark Night of the Soul*, especially chapter VI, for a fuller analysis.

# Chapter X

## ETERNAL LIFE

*T*HE ONE WHOLLY inescapable fact for every human being is that he must die.[1] In this fact man shares the lot of every living creature—but with a difference. Animals, like human beings, have a biological urge to live; they fight tenaciously for life for themselves, and in the higher forms, for their young. But so far as can be observed, animals below man have no vision of the future which would lead them either to long for death or to create a philosophy of resistance to it. Animals do not commit suicide, nor do they yearn for immortality.

It is man's glory that death for him is far more than a biological event. Try as he may to make it purely a physical fact, his higher spiritual impulses refuse to accept it as such. It means the cutting off, or the continuance, of all that is most precious to him, and he must have an answer. Hence the necessity of a faith, and the appearance of belief in immortality in all the great religions of mankind.

Ordinarily the fear of death does not trouble us much; for death, though known to be inevitable, seems a long way off. When serious illness, accident, the death of

---

[1] Some passages in this chapter are reprinted from the chapter entitled "The Shadow of Death" in *The Dark Night of the Soul*.

someone who is loved, or the cheapness of life in war, forces one to think about the transiency of human existence, complacency is no longer possible. One is disturbed, not so much by fear as by a great wonder and confusion. The Christian gospel must say something about it which has the ring of assurance, or it cannot get the ear of the many whose primary, unvoiced question is, "If a man die, shall he live again?"

## 1. *The view of science*

Let us first look briefly at what can be said about immortality from the viewpoints of science.

So scientifically minded is our age that most people would like to have proof of personal immortality if they could have it. This is what gives vogue to experiments in "psychic research" and sends people running to spiritualist séances. The results as yet do not justify any great confidence in spirit communication, though it is as dogmatic to deny its possibility as it is gullible prematurely to affirm it.

The more common allegedly scientific attitude is to deny the possibility of the continuance of personality beyond the life span of the body. The evidence we have in this life seems to indicate that mind and body are so interdependent that there is no mind-state without its accompanying body-state. Let the body cease to function, and all that we call mind, soul, spirit, consciousness, psyche, ego, personality, must cease with it. This seems the simple, even if unwelcome, conclusion of the most elementary knowledge of psychology.

But does it? The fact that there is no agreement among scientists, including psychologists and even great psychologists, should forestall a too hasty conclusion. If all there is of spirit or consciousness is the behavior of the body—that is to say, if mind is the activity of the brain and nervous system in the same sense in which breathing is the activity of the lungs—the only logical conclusion is that it ceases with the death of the body. But to make this affirmation about mind or spirit is to go far beyond the evidence.

In this life—whatever may be true of the next—the mind is experienced in a different way from the body. Ideas, feelings, intentions, and aspirations—all that we ordinarily call thoughts—are quite different from a physical substance such as the brain. Our thoughts we know from looking into our own minds; a brain is seldom observed except in brain surgery, or as one may happen to see or handle the brain of a dead person. Our thoughts doubtless always have some bodily accompaniment, and it is obvious that they often affect the way the body acts. But the thoughts themselves occupy no space; they are invisible, intangible, and of a different order of existence from the motions of matter in space.

Furthermore, the mind does not always seem the passive result of the action of the body. It is easy to point to cases of mental disturbance through injuries to the body. But over against these must be set many instances of spiritual victory over diseased and crippled and pain-racked bodies through sheer will power. In

137

many forms of illness, physical as well as mental, one's state of mind makes a great difference in recovery. To a large degree life consists in making our bodies do what our interests and our choices dictate. Usually without our realizing it, the spirit fashions even the physical appearance of the body, and this is why it is possible to read character in a human face.

There are other more theoretical considerations pointing to the real existence of mind or spirit. If bodily activity is all there is of mind, there is nothing in this to account for the meanings we attach to words, or for their use in a series to make a meaningful sentence, or for the relation of the ideas denoted by them to make a connected body of thought. Even a theory of physiological psychology requires something more than physiology to account for the mental reflections by which this theory can be formulated! If we assume the existence of the body as the *only* source of what we commonly call thought, there remains no way to compare two thoughts to decide which one is truer than the other. Any theory that denies the reality of mind thus refutes itself.

Thus we are led to the conclusion that the mind or spirit of man, though in this life always connected with a body and interacting with it, is by no means identical with the body and is not its powerless product. The mind uses the body here as its vehicle of expression. It could have another medium after death. But of what actually happens beyond this life we have no scientific knowledge.

The truly scientific attitude is to refuse to make assumptions beyond what the evidence warrants. And we do not have the evidence by which either to prove or disprove what happens after death. All that psychology has access to is *living* consciousness and the behavior of the psychological organism in this world. What lies beyond is a proper enough sphere for philosophy or religion, but science stops short of making pronouncements on what, by the nature of the case, it cannot get the evidence upon. This is why the scientists are divided, and the greater scientists are inclined to leave the door open.

## 2. *The view of philosophy*

Though immortality is not so common a theme in philosophy as in religion, many philosophers, past and present, have felt impelled to reckon with it. Naturalistic philosophies tend usually to dismiss it, or to try to find a substitute in the biological continuity of the human race or the social continuity of the influence one leaves behind. It is doubtful whether either of these substitutes ought to be called immortality, for they make no provision for what is central to the whole idea, namely, the preservation of the individual person. Furthermore, there is no assurance that either biological life or social influence will go on indefinitely upon this planet, and this uncertainty has been greatly increased by the coming of the atomic bomb.

Idealistic philosophies in general find belief in personal immortality necessary to complete one's under-standing of personality in this life. They tend to regard it, not as a demonstrated fact, but as an assumption consistent with the view that man is a spiritual being with a high moral destiny.

Personal immortality is closely related to what philosophy calls the "conservation of values." While life lasts, everybody prizes something. Most of us prize many things—friends, family, work, knowledge, beauty, love, God. "What men live by," said Dr. Richard L. Cabot in a famous book by that title, are work, play, love, and worship. Of course we actually prize many other things, such as material possessions, indulgence of the body, the desire to show off and to lord it over others, which in our saner and higher moments we know we should be as well off without. These we could surrender at death without loss. But what of the truly great values—the good, the true, the beautiful, the holy? These exist in persons, and as we seek after them they become part of us—the most important part, by far, of our personalities. They ought not to perish with the death of the body. There ought to be a chance to go on with the quest, and to come to fuller attainments than we can possibly reach in this brief span of life. Many philosophies and most religions hold that such values and the persons who bear them do not perish, "but have everlasting life" in a higher, purer realm.

But how? There are some who believe that as these values come from God they go back to him, and the individual perishes. The logic of this position is that God simply uses human beings as pawns in a cosmic drama, as candles that burn brightly for an hour. This is not the view of the Christian faith. The God of Christianity is one who loves and prizes men for their own sakes, and who could not be content either to shatter precious values or the persons in whose souls these values are borne and cherished. Indeed, of all values, persons are themselves the supreme value and must survive.

### 3. *The view of Christian faith*

Science can say nothing, philosophy something, on the problem of death. We are driven to religion for any ultimate answer.

Why has personal immortality occupied so central a place in Christian faith? There are a number of reasons. For one thing, Christianity was born in the resurrection experience of the early disciples. Shattered in spirit at the loss of their leader, they were about to go back to their homes and fishing nets, saying sadly, "We hoped that it was he who should redeem Israel." Then something happened! It convinced them beyond doubt that their leader was not dead but was in their midst as their living Saviour. "Now is Christ risen from the dead." "Because I live, ye shall live also." "O death, where is thy sting? O grave, where is thy victory? . . . Thanks be to God, which giveth us the victory through our Lord Jesus Christ." As we saw in chapter six, such words

141

became the rallying cry of the fellowship that formed the Christian Church. Thence came faith and hope. They are still words of high assurance to the great company of Christ's followers. What they say eternally to the Christian is, "Though men may do their worst, God reigns victorious over sin and death."

But this is not our only witness. Even without the record of Christ's resurrection, Christianity would in all probability have made personal immortality a central tenet of its faith. It belongs with the kind of God and the understanding of man which Jesus not only taught but demonstrated.

It is the Christian faith that God is our Father. It is irrational to suppose that a God of fatherly love and sustaining power, who has made man in his own image and who loves all men as his children, could let men's lives be abruptly cut off without hope. A God who would let millions of helpless victims of war, and others dying of starvation in time of peace, be snuffed out utterly would not be the God of Jesus. Nor would he be the God even of our own best human insights. A God able to make us is able to preserve us. A God good enough to give us this present life, mixed as it is, can be trusted to complete it in a better one. Without immortality there is no real answer to the brevity of human existence or the unmerited pain that ranges throughout the life we know.

There are many who say they do not care greatly for immortality for themselves and who doubt their own worthiness to survive. This judgment may be prompted by either pessimism or humility. But, leaving this question aside, for no one can be fully objective about himself, can one say this about another whom he loves? The fact is, he cannot. Nor about humanity in general, if one puts upon human personality the estimate of Christian faith. Man is not "like the beasts that perish," and, however much men may treat other men as beasts, we know through Christ that God cannot. Because man is God's supreme creation, a creature of infinite worth and dignity, it is irrational to suppose God shatters ruthlessly his handiwork. And because with all our faults and frailties we are still God's children, we can know our destinies are safe within his enduring care.

Of the many things outside the Bible that have been written on immortality, none has put the case more aptly than this great passage from Tennyson's *In Memoriam:*

> Thou wilt not leave us in the dust:
>     Thou madest man, he knows not why;
>     He thinks he was not made to die;
> And thou hast made him: thou art just.

Were there no other reason for believing in immortality, the goodness of God is reason enough.

## 4. *The nature of the future life*

Regarding the precise nature of the immortal life we must not be too bold. God has not revealed to us the

143

whole mystery. We now see many things "through a glass darkly," and must wait for more light until we see him "face to face." To try to make mental or verbal pictures of the life after death is to run the risk both of letting the imagination run away with us and of introducing very earthy factors into the description. We are simply too space-bound to picture what is not a spatial but a spiritual form of existence. Nevertheless, there are some things we can say about it which are both logical and Christian.

It is consistent with what we know of God through Christ to believe that in the life beyond there will be continuance of the individual soul, fellowship with those we love, a lifting of earthly chains of pain and suffering, a chance to grow in the things of Christ, the glory of God's nearer presence. Each of these beliefs can be thought without having to draw on the imagination. Without the continuance of the individual there would be no immortality, and this carries with it the continuance of the individual's memories, his loves, his ideas and ideals, and all the spiritual qualities that most fully make him what he is. Without fellowship personality would no longer be the social thing we know it to be wherever personality exists. If earthly impediments were not removed, the afflictions of this life could not give place to what Paul calls "a far more exceeding and eternal weight of glory." If growth could not go on, the urge to improve, which is central to man's moral and spiritual nature, would be thwarted; and much of the reason for God's preservation of the soul would vanish with it. If we could not come intimately and gloriously into fellowship with God, the future life would be barren of that which in this life most enriches it.

Just how these things can come about we do not know. It seems plausible to believe that in the next life, as in this, there is a medium of communication, and Paul may not have been wrong when he spoke of "celestial bodies" and "bodies terrestrial." In any case the God who gives us our present bodies can give us others if we need them. Though we should like to know much more and be able to "understand all mysteries," if we can have the assurance of God's care for our loved ones and ourselves, it is all we need.

## 5. *Heaven and hell*

In the chapter "Salvation" we promised to say something more about its meaning in relation to the future life. Salvation through Christ is both for this life and the next, and it is a mistake to locate it solely in either to the exclusion of the other.

Our best clue to the meaning of this is found in the Gospel of John, where the author uses the term "eternal life" to mean, not merely extension of existence beyond the grave, but a quality of life that begins here and is deathless. God so loved the world that he gave his Son, "that whosoever believeth on him should not perish, but have eternal life." This does not mean that the person without Christ perishes at death only, but that he lacks the fullness and richness of eternal life that could be his all along the way. In the great words, "I am the way, the truth, and the life," and "I am the resurrection, and the life," the emphasis is on the new quality of life that can come to the person who makes Christ the center of his faith and loyalty. To be saved by Christ means to enter now into a fellowship with God in Christ that transforms this life and reaches into eternity.

This suggests what we ought to mean by heaven. Heaven has traditionally been thought of as a realm of perfect bliss and rest, in which all the unrequited good deeds done in this life receive their reward. If immortality means what was suggested in the previous section, it is indeed a realm of joy. But the emphasis ought to be, not on reward, but on the joy of fellowship with God and on the opportunity to go on serving him and growing in our own spirits toward "the measure of the stature of the fulness of Christ." Death then means neither the end of life nor the beginning of salvation, but an open door to a larger, fuller life with the Father.

But what of hell? Though there is much imagery in the New Testament to suggest eternal life, outer darkness, weeping, wailing, and gnashing of teeth, the meaning of hell as eternal torment does not fit the loving God whom Jesus taught us to worship. No sensitive person could really be happy in paradise and think of other human beings writhing miserably in eternal fires—and if we cannot, surely God cannot! This has caused a shift from the traditional view that sinners burn in hell, and the idea no longer has a prominent place in modern Protestant thought.

Nevertheless, there is something in the idea of hell that ought not to be given up. What the idea really stands for is: (1) that it makes a difference whether or not we accept salvation through the mercy of God; (2) that if we do not repent and turn from our sin, we must suffer the consequences; (3) that there comes a time when we have sinned away the freedom we once had; and (4) that in hell we have cut ourselves off from awareness of the presence of God. All these conditions occur when we persist in sin in the present life, and can all too frequently be seen in the lives of individuals and social groups.

Just as to follow Christ means entrance now into God's eternal Kingdom, so to reject Christ and disregard his moral demands is to plunge ourselves into hell and drag others with us. One of the things God has been trying to teach us through the colossal suffering of war is that we cannot flout his ways without kindling the fires of conflict that lead to misery and "outer darkness." Within such conflict our freedom greatly shrinks; and though God never forsakes his human children, he is often veiled from sight. What is so clearly true of this life may well be true of the next. As heaven begins but does not end with the life on earth, so the warping and crippling of human spirits through sin probably is not ended with death. "Whatsoever a man soweth, that shall he also reap"—in this life or the next. In just what manner hell extends into the next life we do not know, but if we take seriously the need of obeying God's holy will, we must be equally serious about the consequences of disobedience.

There is a sense in which we make our own heaven and hell. There is another—and deeper—sense in which God gives us the destiny we choose. This sobering thought should bring us both warning and great hope. Some things in the traditional beliefs about heaven and hell we can afford to let go, or leave as we must in the realm of mystery. What we must not surrender is faith in the living, loving, righteous God of Jesus. If our trust is in him, we shall know that for time and eternity our souls are in his keeping, and he has work for us to do.

## Chapter XI

# THE CHRISTIAN IN SOCIETY

GOD IN CREATING us placed us in a great society for fellowship with other human beings. The fact that we live in such a society not only gives us great satisfactions, such as friendship and the joys of family life, but places on us great obligations. The Christian's moral task centers in the very difficult two-fold obligation to love God supremely and our neighbor as ourselves. To the degree that men, by God's help, live up to this demand, God's Kingdom comes on earth. Within the total social scene in which we are called of God to work with him for the advancement of his Kingdom, the Church is a special fellowship with a unique mission. To talk about the Christian in society involves, then, a discussion of Christian ethics, the Kingdom of God, and the Church. In reverse order, we shall take a brief look at each of these great themes.

## 1. *The Church*

The Christian Church is a fellowship of persons united by a common loyalty to Christ and by a desire to worship and do the will of God as revealed in Christ. Let us take this as a preliminary definition and see what it suggests.

First, the Church is a fellowship. It is always composed

of a group, however small. It started with the twelve disciples, grew soon to one hundred and twenty and then to three thousand, and now numbers many millions around the world. Where "two or three are gathered together in my name," there Christ is—or can be—in his Church. Christianity is not, and never has been, a solitary faith. When one asks, "Does one need to go to church to be a Christian?" he is putting the question the wrong way around. One might better say, "If one is a Christian, will he not wish to unite with other Christians in public worship?"

The Christian Church is, of course, only one of many fellowships in existence. There is fellowship—or "community," as some prefer to call it—in a Boy Scout troop, a football team, a school, a woman's club, a Rotary Club, a labor union. This means that, however diverse in other respects, there is a common interest that holds the group together. In the Christian Church, in spite of its many denominations (there are 256 in the United States alone!), there is a common loyalty to Christ which binds the groups together into one. When this central loyalty is lost, as sometimes happens, the Church is no longer a church but a secular club not very different from any other group. The Church is the carrier of the gospel of Christ; when it fails to be this, it is just one more social institution.

This leads us to say, in the second place, that the Church is not only a fellowship but an institution. It is the institutional side of it—organization, forms of government, traditional practices, and patterns of worship—that gives the Church a systematic structure through which to work. Like the body which gives the soul a vehicle of expression, the institution is very necessary to the fellowship but sometimes also very troublesome. The Church as an institution is conservative, and often is marred by human selfishness and eagerness for power. The Church as a fellowship is also human and therefore far from perfect, but in the message of Christ that gives the fellowship its reason for existing lies divine strength and a continual challenge to be more Christlike. It is important therefore that not the institution, but the fellowship with its God-given message, be always kept in the foreground.

Third, the distinctive function of the Church is to help people to worship God. This is why the service of public worship on Sunday is so central. Other agencies have "worship services"; only the Church makes worship primary. Such worship should of course carry over into private prayer and encourage more Christlike living all through the week. The Church has many other services to render—to promote religious education and growth of character, to comfort the sorrowing, to minister to the sick, to counsel those in need, to cultivate world friendship and understanding—in short, to make the power of God available for every human situation. But if it neglects its central task of leading the people in worship, it will lack the power to do much in these other fields. It is a mistake, on the one hand, to make worship in the Church an emotional or aesthetic luxury unrelated to the hard requirements of Christian living; it is a mistake, on the other hand, to suppose that the Church can make the world better unless its people are brought through worship into a vital encounter with God.

Our fourth point is that the Church exists to help men to do the will of God as revealed in Christ. This means the increase of love in human relations. What this ethical obligation involves we shall presently examine in more detail. It applies both to relations with one's family, friends, and close associates and to the vastly more complex relationships of nations, races, cultures, and conflicting economic groups. The Church has accomplished more in the cultivation of love and enlightened good will in the first field than in the second. Nevertheless, because of its social impact through the centuries, the world is a very different place from what it otherwise would have been.

To take a rapid look backward, in the Middle Ages it was the Church that made society stable and kept the torch of learning from going out; it was the medieval faith in a rational God that laid the foundations for modern science; it was the Church that gave rise, in the early days of our country, to great numbers of our colleges. Not all humanitarian service or social progress has come through the Church. But it is the Church more than any other institution which has taught the supreme worth of every person, out of which has come care for the weak and the helpless, the abolition of slavery, the lifting of the position of women and of children, the establishment of hospitals and many social agencies, the challenging of injustice, and the creation of that world-mindedness which is the true foundation of peace. In our time the Church in Europe boldly resisted tyranny and in spite of persecution and martyrdom did more than any other agency to keep democracy alive. Around the world the Church became a community uniting in a spiritual fellowship the people of nations at war with one another, and it is now in the forefront of movements toward relief, reconstruction, and international co-operation. To say that intolerance and compromise in the Church have sometimes thwarted progress is the truth, but to say that these have mainly been the influence of the Church is to stand the truth upon its head.

These facts ought not to be overlooked by critics of the Church, many of whom do not go to church and so have too little knowledge of its life and work to speak accurately about it. Nevertheless, any church which fails to examine itself and purge its own life of snobbery, race prejudice, narrowness, and self-righteousness is hardly the most effective instrument of God's will. Those on the outside of the Church are prejudiced when they see only its flaws and pass it by in disdain; those within it must be sensitive to its (their) faults if they are to speak a prophetic word against the sins of society. What one has to do as a member of the Church—whether layman or minister—is to believe greatly in the Church as the carrier of God's message of salvation, yet be humbly aware of the shortcomings of the weak and sinful human instruments God uses in his work.

Finally, it may be helpful to define some terms often used with reference to the Church. In the Apostles' Creed we say, "I believe in *the holy catholic Church.*" This does not mean the Roman Catholic Church, but the divinely grounded, universal Church of Christ in the whole world. In the war years, the fidelity of Christians in many lands under persecution and great suffering, and the maintaining of the fellowship of the World Church in the face of terrific odds, have given new meaning to this ancient phrase. The Church, having its center in God, is above all nations, races, and classes, and therefore is able to unite the people of the most varied social groups. What it means to be a holy catholic Church is admirably stated in the words of a familiar hymn:

> In Christ there is no East or West,
> In him no South or North;
> But one great fellowship of love
> Throughout the whole wide earth.

The term "ecumenical church," though it goes back to the early centuries of the Christian era, has been revived in recent years to mean the Christian Church of all denominations and nations, or the World Church. As the term is generally used, it means the Protestant and Eastern Orthodox churches, for the Roman Catholic Church prefers not to affiliate with this movement. Through the World Council of Churches, the International Missionary Council, and other agencies its work has gone forward toward greater unity in spite of the barriers and strains of war. When the outbreak of war in Europe cut off financial support from many mission stations—the so-called "orphaned missions"—the Christians of the rest of the world gave the money to keep them going. When missionaries had to be withdrawn from Korea, Japan, and much of China, native Christians carried on the work. Chaplains have ministered on an ecumenical basis both to the armed forces and to millions of prisoners of war. Through study, the spread of information, visits of Christian leaders, the giving of material relief, and most of all through prayer and a fellowship of suffering, a sense of spiritual kinship has been furthered among the Christians of the world. One may well believe that there was something providential in the emergence of the ecumenical movement in the Church just as the world was falling apart.

A great phrase used by Paul, and by Christians ever since, to designate the Church is "the body of Christ." One should read the twelfth chapter of First Corinthians to get the setting. There are diversities of gifts, but the same Holy Spirit; diversities of forms of service, but the same God. As a human body is one but has many members that must work together, so the Church, with all the diversities in its membership, is one body. The passage has its keynote in, "Now ye are the body of Christ, and severally members thereof." The term is a wonderfully descriptive figure of speech, for it emphasizes both the unity of many persons with separate functions within the Church and the fact that it is the presence of the Spirit of Christ that makes a group of ordinary people a Church.

When we wish to stress the unity of the Church, which embraces in its fold the faithful of all ages, the living and the dead, we call it "the communion of saints." The saints, in the Protestant view, are not merely those canonized by the Church, and they are not sinless. They are the dedicated souls who have "fought a good fight and kept the faith"—souls who have lived for God and advanced his cause; souls with whom, in spite of differences of time and place and achievement, we can feel a great kinship of devotion. If for "communion of saints" we substitute mentally "the fellowship of the faithful," the term becomes clearer and emphasizes what is set forth magnificently in the eleventh chapter of Hebrews—the "cloud of witnesses" with which we are "compassed about."

Many other terms have been used to describe the Church. We must, however, move on to say something about that which the Church exists to serve, the Kingdom of God.

## 2. *The Kingdom*

There is nothing in Christian theology about which there is more disagreement among serious-minded students than the meaning of the Kingdom of God. All agree that it was the central message of Jesus. If we open the New Testament to almost any place in the first three Gospels, we find parables of the Kingdom and other references to its coming. We should expect, therefore, that it would be easy enough to discover what he was talking about. However, there are so many recorded sayings about the Kingdom, some of them apparently contradictory, that various theories have been developed as to what Jesus really meant by it, and what we should mean.

It will not be useful here to go into all the fine distinctions as to these theories. One view, held by the premillenialists, puts the emphasis on the physical second coming of Christ, and holds that the Kingdom will come when Christ returns. Another view agrees with this in holding that the Kingdom will come only when God intervenes to put an end to the course of history as we know it, but it puts the Kingdom wholly in another world instead of on earth. Both of these positions get their authority from the apocalyptic passages in the New Testament, which seem to predict the end of this earthly scheme of things by a sudden, dramatic act of God.

A very different view centers in Jesus' saying, "The kingdom of God is within you." It regards the Kingdom as already present in the lives of redeemed individuals to whom Christ has come with transforming power. People who hold this view do not usually look for a physical second coming, but believe that Christ comes to men in spirit, as God's greatest gift, whenever they will receive him. This has been stated admirably in Phillips Brooks' Christmas hymn:

> How silently, how silently
>     The wondrous Gift is given!
> So God imparts to human hearts
>     The blessings of his heaven.
> No ear may hear his coming,
>     But in this world of sin,
> Where meek souls will receive him still,
>     The dear Christ enters in.

Still another view of the Kingdom is that of a Christianized society in which justice and love will prevail—a Kingdom not yet achieved but which men must work for with great earnestness. The Kingdom thus becomes the main incentive to a social gospel. This, too, may be typified by the words of a hymn:

> Rise up, O men of God!
>     His kingdom tarries long;
> Bring in the day of brotherhood
>     And end the night of wrong.[1]

This social interpretation of the Kingdom, which scarcely anyone held before the nineteenth century, has been so widely advocated, particularly in America, that by many it is regarded as *the* doctrine of the Kingdom.

What shall we make of these views? The last two can

[1] William P. Merrill. Used by permission.

be combined, for both look at the coming of the Kingdom as a gradual process taking place here on earth. The salvation of the individual and of society need not—in fact, must not—be separated, and in both man has a definite responsibility. The first two views are on a very different basis, for they despair of the salvation of this world and hold that God, in his own good time, will do whatever needs to be done about bringing in the next.

Probably Jesus shared with others of his time the apocalyptic expectation of a speedy end of the world. Most biblical scholars believe that he did. However, if one takes his message as a whole, it is clear that his main emphasis lies elsewhere. The note he was always urging was the need of dependence on God and obedience to God in all the relations of life, that God's Kingdom might come and his will be done on earth as it is in heaven.

The central meaning of the Kingdom is the righteous, loving rule of God. God demands allegiance like a king; he loves us like a father. If one takes the rule of God as the keynote, many otherwise contradictory passages can be harmonized. The rule of God is already present, yet it must come in the fullness of time when men repent and seek to do God's will on earth. It comes in this world, but the final victory of God's rule lies, not on earth, but in a realm beyond this world. It grows gradually and almost imperceptibly, like leaven or mustard seed; it comes suddenly, like a thief in the night, or the bridegroom at a wedding, and one must be ready and on the watch. "It is the Father's good pleasure to give you the kingdom," yet he gives it to him who, prizing it like a pearl of great price or a treasure hid in the field, gives for it all that he has.

Not all the things that have been believed by Christians about the Kingdom can be reconciled, but the heart of them can be. This was done at the world missionary conference at Madras in words that are worth quoting:

> The Kingdom of God is both present and future; both a growth and a final consummation by God. It is our task and our hope—our task which we face with the power of Christ; our hope that the last word will be spoken by God and that that last word will be victory. The Kingdom means both acceptance and action, a gift and a task. We work for it and we wait for it.[2]

Whether the social meaning of the Kingdom is a right interpretation depends on whether we base our judgment on what Jesus directly said, or on what may be implied from what he said and did. There is little doubt that he was mainly concerned with individuals rather than with social systems. Though he says much in condemnation of selfishness, greed, hypocrisy, and the like, there is no direct word in his recorded sayings about slavery, war, or the political oppression rampant in his day. But this does not mean that no social application can be drawn from his words. Everywhere and al-

[2] *The World Mission of the Church*, p. 106.

ways he believed in persons and—whatever men might think—treated them with the love and respect due a child of God. To the extent that we take seriously these two factors, the righteous rule of God and Jesus' estimate of persons, we are bound to do all we can to remove the barriers that cripple and warp and hamper our brothers in the family of God. Only so can God's Kingdom come and his will be done on earth.

The social gospel is justified, not in the sense that by it we ourselves can "build the Kingdom," but in the obligation to be God's servants in removing obstacles to the abundant life he waits to give. As long as poverty, ignorance, disease, race prejudice, exploitation, oppression, and war remain, God's will for persons cannot be fully done. The best analogy for our relation to the Kingdom is not that of a builder, but the sower of whom Jesus spoke in one of his greatest parables. It is our job to sow the seed and if possible remove the rocks and thorns that choke it; it is God who brings forth the fruit from good ground, some thirty-, some sixty-, some a hundredfold.

### 3. Christian action

We come now to the question which in some respects is the hardest of all, but which nobody who tries seriously to be a Christian can evade. How can we know the will of God? And if we know it, can we do it?

As to how to know the will of God, two warnings are necessary at the outset. First, we must not be so sure we know it that we shall be intolerant of equally sincere Christians who think differently. Second, we must be sure enough that we know it to go ahead with confidence. As in all search for the truth, we must combine open-mindedness and a teachable spirit with convictions to live by. The combination is not easy, but it is essential if we are not to be bigoted or to flounder in uncertainties.

If we are to know the will of God in a decision we have to make, such as what vocation to choose, how to deal with a difficult person, what to do about war, several things are necessary. They are not easy. Briefly stated, they are these: (1) We must learn the mind of Christ. (2) We must let ourselves be led by the Holy Spirit. (3) We must view the situation in its total setting, and particularly the consequences. (4) We must act by the light we have.

In order to "let this mind be in you, which was also in Christ Jesus," as Paul put it, it is necessary to live with the New Testament until it becomes a part of us. There is no single passage, not even such great ones as the Sermon on the Mount or the magnificent hymn of love in the thirteenth chapter of First Corinthians, that says it all. There is no rule, not even the Golden Rule, that can be applied automatically. Yet there is a spirit of devotion to God and love for men, pervading the accounts of the life and words and works of Jesus, that is the indispensable basis of any Christian action.

In the second place, we must pray and be open to the

leading of the Holy Spirit. The Holy Spirit, or the Spirit of God, is that continuing, indwelling presence of God which we could be aware of at all times if we were not too dull to sense this presence. When we pray, if we pray humbly and receptively as we should, we let down the barriers and listen to the voice of God. The answer comes, sometimes in overwhelmingly clear convictions, sometimes in dim intuitions of the direction in which to move. Such answers can be taken as God's leading only if we are careful to make God's will, and not our own wishes, determine the current of our praying. Often we are left with a great deal of thinking yet to do.

In the third place (not third in time, for all these steps should proceed together), we must look as clearly, as widely, and as fair-mindedly at the situation as we can. Here the help of a trusted counselor, one's pastor, family, or friends, is often very valuable. Nobody can decide the question for us, but often someone else can point out consequences we have not seen or thought about. It is essential that one ask which of the possible courses of action will do the most good, not to oneself only, but to all the persons who may be affected by it. One has to reckon with the fact that to do the most Christlike thing may bring suffering to oneself and to those one loves. One ought not to shrink from a cross, but neither ought one to court martyrdom simply for the sake of feeling noble.

Finally, having made as Christian a decision as is possible under the circumstances, one must go ahead by the light he has, awaiting more. "If any man willeth to do his will, he shall know of the teaching, whether it is of God." Without such decision, life grows flabby and lacks the purpose that spiritual health and wholeness require. God may continue to prick the conscience when we do wrong, but before long a vision disregarded fades away.

But, having discovered what we sincerely believe to be the will of God for us in our time and place and circumstances, can we do it? The answer is both yes and no. We can set our faces toward the right, pray for God's help as we go forward, and accomplish much. This must be said in reply to those who believe that, because Christianity demands an impossible perfection, it is a beautiful but impractical ideal. For the past two thousand years people who have tried to do the will of God as revealed in Christ have made a great difference in the world, both through the strength and radiance of their own lives and their impact on their times. Most of the morally and spiritually constructive movements of history have stemmed from this source. There is no reason now to give up trying.

On the other hand, it is a mistake to suppose that any of us will ever do perfectly the will of God. In the most dedicated Christian, there are always enough roots of self-love to keep him humble and in need of continual repentance. There have been—and there still are—Christian saints, but no real saint ever thinks of himself as one because he knows too well his need of

God's forgiveness. The most effective Christian life is that of the person who, distrusting his own righteousness, trusts God enough to go forward in spite of his limitations.

Must every moral decision involve choosing "the lesser of two evils"? Many believe so, and in a sense it is true, for life comes mixed with evil elements. But if we turn the phrase around, we shall have something that in reality is much truer. Every choice is between *a greater and a lesser good*, and we ought to choose the greater. The difference between this and "the lesser of two evils" lies in the fact that the greater good means the more Christlike course of action. We have, then, not merely to choose between conflicting evils. The more important fact is that in these choices, we must—and can—have a perfect goal to steer by and a perfect source of power to draw upon. This is far more than a verbal difference. Whether we believe that Christianity can save the world in its present tangle of evil forces depends much on the degree to which we keep the goal in view and try humbly to draw upon this Power.

## Chapter XII

## CHRISTIAN FAITH AND THE PRESENT CRISIS

*T*HROUGHOUT THE PRECEDING chapter we have dealt, for the most part, with ideas which require no date. If they are true, they are true for every time. However, it will be appropriate in conclusion to note the bearing of these Christian convictions on some of the problems which now confront us.

There are two dates of outstanding importance in the history of mankind. One is the turning point of all history, the date from which we reckon our calendars, the birth of Jesus Christ. On that occasion a person came into the world who has been the most potent force for the healing and reconcilation of the world that mankind has seen. The other date is nearer to the present—so near that not all of us have as yet fully grasped its meaning. It is August 6, 1945. When the first atomic bomb was dropped on Hiroshima, forces were unleashed which may mean the end of human existence, and which in any case present a menace to human security and welfare which few had dreamed of.

Some years ago H. G. Wells made the arresting statement that "civilization is a race between education and catastrophe." We can now go further and say, as many scientists, educators, and journalists, as well as religious leaders are saying, that human existence itself is now in a race between good will and catastrophe. The fate of mankind on this planet hangs in the balance between what Christ stands for and what the bomb stands for.

Let us take a look at three passages, two from the Bible and one from our own time.

In the thirtieth chapter of Deuteronomy we read:

See, I have set before thee this day life and good, and death and evil; in that I command thee this day to love the Lord thy God, to walk in his ways, and to keep his commandments and his statutes and his judgments, that thou mayest live and multiply. . . . But if thine heart turn away, so that thou wilt not hear, but shalt be drawn away, and worship other gods, and serve them; I denounce unto you this day, that ye shall surely perish. . . . I call heaven and earth to record this day against you, that I have set before you life and death, blessing and cursing: therefore choose life, that both thou and thy seed may live.[1]

The second passage contains the familiar words of the first Christmas carol:

And suddenly there was with the angel a multitude of the heavenly host praising God, and saying,
    "Glory to God in the highest,
        And on earth peace among men in whom he is well pleased." [2]

[1] Deuteronomy 30:15-19.
[2] Luke 2:13.

The third is from the words of General MacArthur in Tokyo Bay on the deck of the battleship "Missouri":

We have had our last chance. . . . The problem basically is theological and involves a spiritual recrudescence and improvement of human character that will synchronize with our almost matchless advance in science, art, literature and all material and cultural developments of the past two thousand years. It must be of the spirit if we are to save the flesh.

These passages need little elaboration. The first is an Old Testament insight expressed in words attributed to Moses, but with a truth demonstrated over and over again in human history. We can serve God and do his will and live; we can thwart God's will by malice and selfishness, kill one another, and perish. Soon after the first World War, I heard a great English preacher, Dr. G. A. Studdert-Kennedy, say this in words that burned their way into my memory. "You can't buck the universe. It was meant to be a family. If you treat it as a battleground, everybody loses." Everybody lost before. Everybody may lose again—and with more dreadful havoc and destruction—unless with life-and-death seriousness we now choose to do the will and the works of God. God gives us our choice; he may have given us our last chance. He sets before us life and death, the blessing and the curse, and calls us to choose life that we and our children may live.

The second passage in the familiar King James Version reads, "Glory to God in the highest, and on earth peace, good will toward men." In the more accurate translation of the Revised Standard Version we find, "On earth peace among men with whom he is pleased." The meaning is not that God loves some people more than others, and so bestows peace on his favorites. It means, rather, that the God who loves all men is pleased only with the deeds of men of good will. Only by acts and attitudes pleasing to God can we expect to have peace on earth.

When our hope of peace grows fainthearted, let us remember that these words of the Christmas story came not from the shepherds—common folk like us—or even from the wise men, for they were not wise enough to grasp so great a thought. They come from a realm beyond this earth. They come from God himself to say to us in beautiful poetic symbolism, "You *can* have peace. You can have it, not on your terms of vengeance and self-seeking, but on my terms of reconciliation and good will. Give glory to God in the highest in your deeds, and peace will come on earth."

One does not usually go to a secular newspaper for great religious utterances. Yet the Christmas editorial in one of them has put this truth as forcefully as I have seen it. Speaking of our persistent hatred of our enemies after we have defeated them, hundreds of thousands of women and children condemned to death from hunger and cold in Europe, millions of men held in slavery as prisoners of war and forced laborers, little wars that have sprung up in many places after the big wars have ended, the editorial says:

There is no reconstruction because there is no peace; there is no peace because there is no genuine reconciliation. . . . Starvation and freezing, exile, slavery and hopelessness are the portion of our former enemies.

The world will never find peace by this road, but rather new and more terrible wars.

Peace is the reward that comes to men of good will. . . . Hate and the desire for vengeance divide us and threaten us all.[3]

The full force of the quotation from General Mac-Arthur has not yet come home to most people of the churches. "The problem," he says, "basically is theological." "Theology," we have seen, means simply "understanding the Christian faith." The challenge Mac-Arthur puts before us is the oddest thing ever said by a commanding general in the hour of victory—that we must understand our religious faith well enough to put it into operation! "It must be of the spirit if we are to save the flesh," and it cannot wisely be of the spirit unless we know what the spirit of God impels us to do.

The most serious fact that confronts the churches—and thus confronts the world—is the lack of an adequate theology on the part of the laymen. This is not to say that they are irreligious. But much of the effort of the churches is ineffective because the rank and file of the people have not been given any real understanding of what the Christian gospel is and what it means. There are enough Christian laymen to transform society from its present predicament of conflict and insecurity into a scene of harmony, peace, and effective living—if these Christian laymen understood the gospel and took it seriously.

Every Sunday thousands of sermons are preached all over the United States and in the greater part of the Western world. The world goes on very much as if the sermons were not preached! The sermons are good, bad, and indifferent—some of them very good, but even the best of them do not greatly alter what happens during the week. The laymen are the crucial point in society. It is laymen—not in most cases the clergy—whose acts and attitudes determine military policies, peace treaties and settlements, conditions of employment, investment, wages and prices, housing, the availability of food for ourselves and for the hungry, racial equality or discrimination, the news, the movies, recreation, family life, and the whole vast structure of human relations with which every newspaper deals. Since church membership in the United States now includes 52.5 per cent of the total population, a fairly large section of the people of America go to church at least occasionally. That going to church and hearing sermons makes so little difference at vital points is the most appalling fact that confronts us today.

There are many reasons why we go on preaching and

caroling about "peace on earth, good will among men," and doing the things which make for war. There is not only evil will, but ignorance, moral dullness, narrowness of vision, the tendency to identify God with our nation or our own cause, the ever-present impulse as individuals and social groups to think more of ourselves than of anybody else. Beneath all these reasons is the lack of any clear and vital understanding of the Christian faith. "The problem basically is theological"; for while right understanding will not guarantee right action, wrong understanding—or no understanding—with its usual accompaniment of intolerance or indifference can diffuse Christian action, set earnest people working against each other, push religion to the side lines, and hasten the destruction of mankind.

In conclusion, let us see how the Christian understanding of God gives direction for our time.

It is the Chrisitan faith that there is one God who is the Father Almighty, maker of heaven and earth; that he makes exacting moral demands and in mercy offers salvation to those who in repentance turn to him; that he loves and cares for individuals, knows their need and seeks always to help them; that his will may be thwarted, but his purposes are long and his victory sure. God is like Jesus. In the life, the words, the death, and the living presence of Christ we see what God is and how he works with men.

Each of these statements about the nature of God says something about the present crisis.

If God is *one,* he cannot be a tribal or national deity, such as we make of him when we identify his cause with a particular nation or race. He is the one Father of all men; and Germans and Japanese, Hottentots and middle-class Americans, are equally his sons.

If God is *the maker of heaven and earth,* even atomic energy is God's energy. The scientists did not make it; they simply discovered another of God's laws. That which can destroy can also be used to bless and heal mankind. We need to be shaken out of our lethargy by the dangers of atomic energy; we need also to be challenged by it to turn to constructive ends whatever God has placed in the world. His creation is not ended, and we are his servants and co-workers.

If God *makes exacting moral demands,* this gives perspective on both the war and the peace. In the last war, far more clearly than in any previous one, we were able to see it as the judgment of God on our individual and national selfishness.

We cannot sow the wind and not reap the whirlwind. This we can see in retrospect. But we are stone-blind if we do not see that present policies of mass starvation, the attempt to crush the economic life of Germany, the attempt to keep the secret of atomic energy to ourselves, the peacetime conscription of youth for military ends, the perpetuation of imperialism in the Orient, race discrimination here and around the world, the continuance of attitudes of hatred, vengeance, and greed are as surely laying the foundations of future wars as anything that in the past led up to this one. God sets before us life and death; we must choose.

But if God *in mercy offers salvation,* he has not left us without a way of deliverance. This deliverance is through Christ. It comes to us through the loving, strong, stinging, but gentle radiance of the man whose story fills the four Gospels. No one can read that story thoughtfully without being challenged by it to be a better person. Millions have been thus challenged, and this is why by common consent the coming of Jesus into the world is reckoned the turning point in history. Whether we seek to follow his way or only admire it from afar, in him we see the way of love in action and we know that if only men would follow it, life would be different.

But this is not all. We must find Christ not only in the pages of the Bible and as a figure in history, but within us. The thing must happen to us that happened to Paul. When the spirit of Christ gets on the inside of life and we make him the center of our faith and loyalty, we shall find ourselves saying—in other words perhaps—what Paul said: "It is no longer I that live, but Christ liveth in me"; "I can do all things in him that strengtheneth me." When the cross of Christ becomes our cross and his triumph ours, forgiveness becomes easier because we have been forgiven. Along this way of repentance, forgiveness, and daily companionship with Christ lies deliverance from futility and fear.

*If God loves and cares* for individuals, then prayer matters. We cannot expect through prayer alone to bring peace to the world. We must know and do the things that make for peace. But through prayer we can lay hold upon the three things most lacking, and most needed, in our world today—faith, hope, and love. Without these there can be no stable Christian life for the individual and there can be no stable world order.

Confronted by the turmoil of our time, we are not likely to have the faith, the hope, or the love to do much about it. It is easier to let things drift and talk about the badness of it. This is what most people do. But through prayer we can find our direction and our motive power in God. Then we can begin to act, knowing—as the proverb puts it—that "it is better to light a candle in the dark than to curse the darkness."

Finally, if *God's victory is sure,* whatever happens on earth, we need not despair. We must not be indifferent to the peril, the suffering, or the sin in the world. God cares mightily what happens on earth, and we must care. But if men should thwart God's will until the nations had done their worst and atomic energy should destroy us all, it is the Christian's faith that there is an eternal Kingdom in which God's triumph is assured. With this hope of a Kingdom both within and beyond this world, the Christian can keep on praying, loving, hoping, trusting, working.

Upon the carriers of the Christian gospel rests, under God, the outcome of the race between good will and catastrophe. We *can* have peace, security, and the good

life for all men on God's terms; on any other terms we
face destruction so far-reaching and so terrible that
beside it the last war would seem a trifling incident. We
must choose.

"See, I have set before thee this day life and good,
and death and evil; . . . therefore choose life, that both
thou and thy seed may live."

"Glory to God in the highest, and on earth peace."

"The problem basically is theological. . . . It must be
of the spirit if we are to save the flesh."

To these words of warning and promise we must add
a fourth. In it lie our charter of salvation and our sum-
mons to service in a day that is too hard for us, but not
for God.

"God was in Christ, reconciling the world unto himself, not imputing their trespasses unto them; and hath
committed unto us the word of reconciliation."

# SELECTED BIBLIOGRAPHY

**A.** *Popularly written books on Christian beliefs*

A number of the older books in the following list are out of print. I include them because they may still be available in libraries.

Bosworth, Edward I. *What It Means to Be a Christian.* Boston: Pilgrim Press, 1922.

Bowne, Borden P. *Studies in Christianity.* Boston: Houghton Mifflin Co., 1909.

Brown, Charles R. *Why I Believe in Religion.* New York: The Macmillan Co., 1933.

Brown, William Adams. *Beliefs That Matter.* New York: Charles Scribner's Sons, 1928.

Coffin, Henry Sloane. *Some Christian Convictions.* New Haven: Yale University Press, 1915.

Fosdick, Harry Emerson. *Three Meanings: Prayer, Faith, Service.* New York: Association Press, 1917.

——. *Adventurous Religion.* New York: Harper & Bros., 1926.

Gray, Henry David. *A Theology for Christian Youth.* New York and Nashville: Abingdon-Cokesbury Press, 1941.

Harkness, Georgia. *Conflicts in Religious Thought.* New York: Henry Holt & Co., 1929.

——. *The Recovery of Ideals.* New York: Charles Scribner's Sons, 1937.

——. *The Faith by Which the Church Lives.* New York: Abingdon-Cokesbury Press, 1940.

Horton, Walter M. *Our Christian Faith*. Boston: Pilgrim Press, 1945.

Jones, Rufus M. *Pathways to the Reality of God*. New York: The Macmillan Co., 1931.

Knox, John. *The Man Christ Jesus*. Chicago: Willett, Clark & Co., 1941.

Lewis, Edwin. *A Manual of Christian Beliefs*. New York: Charles Scribner's Sons, 1927.

Moran, Hugh. *A Creed for College Men*. New York: The Macmillan Co., 1924.

Palmer, Albert W. *The Light of Faith*. New York: The Macmillan Co., 1945.

Rall, Harris Franklin. *A Faith for Today*. New York: Abingdon-Cokesbury Press, 1936.

Rowland, Eleanor Harris. *The Right to Believe*. Boston: Houghton Mifflin Co., 1909.

Soper, Edmund D. *What May I Believe?* New York: Abingdon Press, 1927.

Swain, Richard LaRue. *What and Where Is God?* New York: The Macmillan Co., 1921.

———. *What and Why Is Man?* New York: The Macmillan Co., 1925.

Van Dusen, Henry P. *In Quest of Life's Meaning*. New York: Association Press, 1926.

Wicks, Robert R. *The Reason for Living*. New York: Charles Scribner's Sons, 1935.

Weston, Sidney, and Harlow, S. Ralph. *Social and Religious Problems of Young People*. New York: Abingdon-Cokesbury Press, 1934.

B. *The Hazen Series*

These small books published by the Hazen Foundation

were written primarily for college students, but in most cases are adapted for use by laymen in the churches. They are obtainable from the Association Press, 347 Madison Avenue, New York, New York, at fifty cents each. The books are listed in the order of their publication.

Bennett, John C. *Christianity—and Our World.*

Lyman, Mary Ely. *Jesus.*
Horton, Walter. *God.*
Harkness, Georgia. *Religious Living.*
Latourette, Kenneth Scott. *Toward a World Christian Fellowship.*
Steere, Douglas. *Prayer and Worship.*
Stewart, George. *The Church.*
Tittle, Ernest Fremont. *Christians in an Unchristian Society.*
Calhoun, Robert L. *What Is Man?*
Vlastos, Gregory. *Christian Faith and Democracy.*
Bowie, Walter Russell. *The Bible.*
Van Dusen, Henry P. *Reality and Religion.*
Lyman, Eugene W. *Religion and the Issues of Life.*

## C. *More advanced treatments*

Hundreds of scholarly works on Christian theology and the philosophy of religion have been written. The following are among the most rewarding, and are not too difficult for the thoughtful layman.

Baillie, John. *The Interpretation of Religion.* New York: Charles Scribner's Sons, 1936.
Bennett, John C. *Social Salvation.* New York: Charles Scribner's Sons, 1935.

——. *Christian Realism*. New York: Charles Scribner's Sons, 1941.

Brightman, Edgar S. *A Philosophy of Religion*. New York: Prentice-Hall, 1940.

Garnett, A. Campbell. *A Realistic Philosophy of Religion*. Chicago: Willett, Clark & Co., 1942.

Hocking, William Ernest. *The Meaning of God in Human Experience*. New Haven: Yale University Press, 1912.

——. *Human Nature and Its Remaking*. New Haven: Yale University Press, 1923.

——. *The Self: Its Body and Freedom*. New Haven: Yale University Press, 1928.

Horton, Walter M. *Theology in Transition*. New York: Harper & Bros., 1943.

——. *Our Eternal Contemporary*. New York: Harper & Bros., 1942.

Knox, John. *Christ the Lord*. Chicago: Willett, Clark & Co., 1945.

Knudson, Albert C. *The Doctrine of God*. New York: Abingdon Press, 1930.

——. *The Doctrine of Redemption*. New York: Abingdon-Cokesbury Press, 1933.

Lewis, Edwin. *God and Ourselves*. New York: Abingdon-Cokesbury Press, 1931.

Lyman, Eugene W. *The Meaning and Truth of Religion*. New York: Charles Scribner's Sons, 1933.

Niebuhr, Reinhold. *The Nature and Destiny of Man*. New York: Charles Scribner's Sons, 1941, 1943, Vols. I and II.

Pittenger, Norman. *Christ and Christian Faith*. New York: Round Table Press, 1941.

Rall, Harris Franklin. *Christianity: An Inquiry into Its*

*Nature and Truth.* New York: Charles Scribner's Sons, 1940.

Rauschenbusch, Walter. *A Theology for the Social Gospel.* New York: The Macmillan Co., 1917.

Robinson, H. Wheeler. *Redemption and Revelation.* New York: Harper & Bros., 1942.

Temple, William. *Nature, Man and God.* London: Macmillan & Co., 1934.

Trueblood, D. Elton. *The Logic of Belief.* New York: Harper & Bros., 1942.

Van Dusen, Henry P. *The Plain Man Seeks for God.* New York: Charles Scribner's Sons, 1935.

—— (ed.). *The Christian Answer.* New York: Charles Scribner's Sons, 1945.

# INDEX

[Arabic numerals refer to pages; italic Roman numerals to chapters]

183

# INDEX

[Arabic numerals refer to pages; italic Roman numerals to chapters]

# INDEX

[Arabic numerals refer to pages; italic Roman numerals to chapters]